ACCESS YOUR ONLINE RESOURCES

Supporting Life Skills for Children and Young People with Vision Impairment and Other Disabilities is accompanied by a number of printable online materials, designed to ensure this resource best supports your professional needs.

Activate your online resources:

Go to www.routledge.com/cw/speechmark and click on the cover of this book.

Click the "Sign in" or "Request Access" button and follow the instructions in order to access the resources.

T0392817

Supporting Life Skills for Children and Young People with Vision Impairment and Other Disabilities

This practical resource is designed to help professionals, parents, and carers on their journey to independence with children and young people with vision impairments.

Building on the ideas and practices introduced in *Supporting Life Skills for Young Children with Vision Impairment and Other Disabilities*, this book addresses middle childhood, the period from when the child starts school, through to the onset of puberty. It offers a wealth of practical strategies and activities to enhance key skills, including personal safety, advanced dressing, personal hygiene, dealing with puberty, social skills, time, money and organisational skills, eating, drinking and food preparation skills, and the transition to secondary school.

This book:

◆ Addresses the main independent living skills areas for vision impaired children in middle childhood, by providing simple explanations of skills and offering practical strategies and techniques to support progression onto the next stage

◆ Is written in a fully accessible style, with photocopiable pages and additional downloadable eResources

◆ Provides a variety of documentation to chart the child's development and show progress over time

◆ This invaluable resource puts the changes that occur during middle childhood into context and will help busy professionals, families, and carers start preparing children with a vision impairment for adulthood, allowing them to become confident and independent individuals.

Fiona Broadley has taught Habilitation Skills (mobility, orientation, and independent living) to children and young people with vision impairments and additional needs for over 30 years. As the Chair of Habilitation VIUK she helped gather research for the Mobility21 Project, which led to the creation of the National Quality Standards for the delivery of Habilitation Training. She currently heads a team of Registered Qualified Habilitation Specialists and lectures at Birmingham City University and the University of Birmingham.

Supporting Life Skills for Children and Young People with Vision Impairment and Other Disabilities

A Middle Childhood Habilitation Handbook

Fiona Broadley

Routledge
Taylor & Francis Group

LONDON AND NEW YORK

Designed cover image: © istock and Fiona Broadley

First published 2023
by Routledge
4 Park Square, Milton Park, Abingdon, Oxon OX14 4RN

and by Routledge
605 Third Avenue, New York, NY 10158

Routledge is an imprint of the Taylor & Francis Group, an informa business

British Library Cataloguing-in-Publication Data
A catalogue record for this book is available from the British Library

ISBN: 978-1-032-24788-5 (hbk)
ISBN: 978-1-032-24789-2 (pbk)
ISBN: 978-1-003-28013-2 (ebk)

DOI: 10.4324/9781003280132

Typeset in Avant Garde
by Deanta Global Publishing Services, Chennai, India
Printed and bound by CPI Group (UK) Ltd, Croydon CR0 4YY

Access the companion website: www.routledge.com/cw/speechmark

Contents

Common terms

Common terms used in this book.

You will refer to the parent, guardian, carer or professional supporting the child.

The use of **he**, **she**, or **they** is interchangeable when referring to the child.

The book will use the term **vision impairment** to refer to a range of different eye conditions affecting vision. A child may be referred to as vision impaired or severely vision impaired which may be abbreviated to **VI** or **SVI**. Occasionally the terms **sight impaired** and **severely sight impaired** may be used as these are the currently accepted terms used on the certificate of vision impairment. These both replace but are synonymous with partially sighted and blind. The abbreviation **CYPVI** refers to Children and Young People with Vision Impairment and is used at multiple points in the book.

Reference may also be made to **tactile learners**. These children are unable to draw any visual information and are dependent on tactile communication learning methods such as **Braille**, **Moon**, on-body signing, etc. It does not necessarily preclude the use of speech. References to children with useful vision or residual vision target those who would benefit from increased contrast or well-saturated colours.

At points references will be made to **PfA – Preparation for Adulthood Outcomes** which may be included in your child's **EHCP – Education Health Care Plan** if they have one. The PfA Outcomes were designed by the DfE following the recommendations to place more emphasis on preparing for adulthood in the **SEND Code of Practice 2014: 0 to 25 Years**. These documents relate specifically to **England**.

In **Scotland** the EHCP equivalent is the **CSP** or **Co-ordinated Support Plan** and in **Wales** it is the **Statement of Special Educational Needs**, although SEN is changing to **ALN – Additional Learning Needs** and each child will have an **Individual Development Plan (IDP)**.

Dual sensory impairment relates to sight and hearing loss.

MDVI stands for **Multiple Disabilities and Vision Impairment** and **MSI** for **Multi-Sensory Impairment**.

Habilitation Training is the term used for the teaching of orientation and mobility and independent living skills or life skills to children and young people with vision impairments.

The Glossary terms at the back of the book also appear in **bold** within the main text.

Part 1

Introduction

Introduction

Whilst there are multi-generational families with vision impairments, for many families, vision impairment is unexpected, frightening, and isolating. This book aims to allay fears and promote positive attitudes. It is designed to support you on your journey with your child roughly from the time they start school through to the onset of puberty, which equates roughly to middle childhood. Middle childhood is generally accepted to be between the ages of 6 and 12 but is less defined for the purposes of this book. Middle childhood is a period of great change and the support your child will need will differ from that necessary in the early years.

The aim is to share a range of practical activities, skills, and strategies which will help a child with vision impairment to be as independent as possible. These are guide landmarks, rather than being age specific, because each child develops at their own pace and needs different things at different times. It is written specifically with parents and carers in mind, as well as being appropriate for the range of professionals who may support your child with vision impairment.

The book is divided into sections covering different topics. The detail of the topic is listed at the start of the section, followed by a list of relevant activity sheets and handouts included in the book, and links to useful websites or books. Some of the activities and diagrams are now designed to be used more easily with tactile learners. Prerequisite skills are identified, but not necessarily addressed in this book. Occasionally you may be referred back to the first book in this series or to external sites.

You should use your own judgement to determine whether the tasks in this book are age or ability appropriate for your child or seek guidance from a **Registered Qualified Habilitation Specialist (RQHS)** or other suitable professional. If your child is not able to achieve a particular skill, it may be that he has missed a prerequisite developmental stage, or he is simply working to his own timeline. These divisions are artificial, created primarily to allow activities to be offered within manageable parameters, if you still have concerns, refer back to the first book in this series, *Supporting Life Skills for Children with Vision Impairment and Other Disabilities: An Early Years Habilitation Handbook*, which may offer more appropriate skills and strategies.

Chronological age is no indicator of maturity, ability, or skill and for some children delays could stem from factors not related to sight impairment. Many of the skills included here are to allow for progression and could also be incorporated into a Life Skills programme for older children and young people. Both this and the earlier book primarily target children and young people with vision impairment. However, a high proportion of children with VI also have additional disabilities and many of these strategies work equally well with children without a vision impairment

DOI: 10.4324/9781003280132-2

who, for whatever reason, have struggled to absorb the necessary skills. Many are particularly suitable for children with autistic spectrum or sensory processing disorders. Much lateral thinking will be needed, because the most obvious way is not always the best. There is no correct way; safety and success are key. Consider each child as an individual and help them achieve as much as they can, safely within their own capabilities.

At this point in a child's development, he needs to experience new challenges, learn to take calculated risks, and become more independent. Wrapping children in cotton wool may make you feel they are safe, but it does not allow them to experience the real world around them and develop and learn from that experience. It is important for everyone involved with the child to push back against **learned helplessness** by practising independence from a young age and by cultivating resilience and self-esteem.

HOW TO USE THIS BOOK

If you thought that now your child had started school your role would diminish and school would deliver all the additional skills that your child will need to become as independent as possible, you may well be disappointed. Whilst things are improving with the advent of the Expanded Core Curriculum (ECC) and the **Curriculum Framework for Children and Young People (CFVI)**, unless your child is in a specialist or special school setting, or in a resource base, the chances are skills teaching time will be lost to the National Curriculum. That said, good support staff, QTVIs and Habilitation Specialists can make an enormous difference to your child's outcomes.

If you feel your child needs more support than they are receiving from the school or Local Authority (LA) look at the LA's **Local Offer** pages to see what else might be available. If after approaching the school or LA for assistance you still have concerns, you may like to contact **SENDIASS**, **IPSEA**, or **SOS!SEN**, or similar organisations for advice.

The lower your child's vision, the more taxing and tiring the school day will be, so pick your time to develop his skills. Weekends and school holidays work better for parents and carers, rather than in the evening after school. Liaise closely with your child's **Habilitation Specialist** or **QTVI** to ensure a consistency of approach. There is nothing more confusing to a child than being told to do a task one way by one person and a completely different way by another. Your vision support team may share information and leaflets about what they are working on, so you can support your child at home. The book does not need you to work through it systematically, but is designed to allow you to dip in and out according to your child's needs at any given time. If your child expresses an interest in something, take the opportunity to develop their skillset.

Most sighted children learn by watching parents and siblings and then modelling behaviour. Children with limited or no vision miss out on this incidental learning and without visual prompts can be at a disadvantage in the learning process.

Encourage independence

Let him try things and don't intervene too soon, but let him develop problem-solving skills when things go wrong. You learn more from things going wrong and figuring out how to do it properly. It helps a child develop confidence, pride and resilience. If you take over too soon there is a risk of **learned helplessness** which can be difficult to undo. That said, don't add pressure by introducing too many new skills or allowing him to struggle under time constraints.

Be patient

Your child will need repetition of tasks in order to succeed. Always allow enough time for each task and time for it to go wrong or repeat without any additional time pressure. If it's a new task, or one your child struggles with, build in an element of success even if the entire task cannot be completed. Break skills down into their smallest component parts in order to better explain them to your child.

There are many different teaching skills and strategies explained in more detail in the glossary. These include **Demonstration**, **Forward chaining**, **Backward chaining**, **Hand over hand**, **Hand under hand**, **Verbal directions**, **Scaffolding**, or a combination thereof.

Offer praise and encouragement

Children thrive on praise, but as the child matures, make sure your praise and encouragement reflect that. Praise effort that the child puts in, not just the success. Beware of continuing to use Motherese, the sing song, exaggerated intonation used with babies and young children, as you child gets older. Focus on the success and plan the task well, so that as your child gains confidence, you can either add more challenges, or withdraw your support. If you introduce your child to household tasks offer suitable incentives or rewards as encouragement.

Be consistent

Avoid your child receiving mixed messages. If there is a method or strategy that works for your child, stick with it, and encourage everyone who works with the child to do the same. Use the same language and terminology across all settings to avoid confusion and share expectations regarding tasks the child should perform independently.

Communicate

Learn how to verbalise what is going on at home, without overwhelming your child. Choose clear descriptive language that helps your child visualise activities. Take the time to explain idiomatic or colloquial language and also the environment around him to build his understanding of the world. Think about body language, gestures, and facial expressions and explain them to the child.

Anyone outside the immediate family should introduce themselves by name. The child also should be addressed by name, so that they are certain conversation is being directed at them. Discourage people from asking the child to guess who they are, it can be confusing and embarrassing on both sides. "Oh, hello Auntie Mabel! I'd recognise that smell anywhere." On the other hand, professionals may do it deliberately in order to teach the child how to respond or develop voice recognition skills.

Your child is likely to be very dependent on verbal description and instruction so help him build his skills and if you have any concerns seek a referral to a **Speech and Language Therapist**. Although children with vision impairment do not have enhanced hearing, they do have the brain capacity to make good use of listening skills and draw more information from auditory sources if they are taught how.

To develop understanding further, don't just tell your child what you are doing, but also allow him hands on experience. "What the hand does, the mind remembers" (Maria Montessori).

If your child needs **objects of reference** or alternative communication systems like Makaton or on body signing, make sure there is a consistency of approach across all settings.

Encourage your child to take responsibility

Seize the moment. If your child expresses interest in a particular task, try and address it there and then, if you can. If not, negotiate a suitable time when you can try it without interruption.

It can be very easy to take the line of least resistance and do things for your child because it's quicker and easier, but your child needs to learn to take responsibility for their own actions. That could include undertaking a task unprompted or allowing themselves enough time to complete the task without help. Look for opportunities to increase the range of activities the child undertakes independently and review it frequently as the child matures. Much of this book is about how to let your child deal independently with the world and preparing yourself and your child for that moment.

As the child progresses, recognise that occasional failure is also a valid option. Accepting and overcoming failure by trying again builds resilience.

Keep it fun

Despite increasing maturity, the child is still just that – a child. Try and make activities fun, offer breaks and variations in the activities to keep the child engaged. Many skills can be developed through games and play without the child being aware of the purpose. At this age children still need to play, both for its own sake, and to continue their development. Most children will still benefit from being read stories to enhance their understanding of the world and build a love of reading, using construction toys to develop hand strength and playing multiplayer games to learn turn-taking and an understanding of losing. For some children early years toys and story bags may continue to be helpful to reinforce understanding and development.

Reach out for help and support

Every child is different; some have complex conditions and medical needs that must be taken into consideration. Find out as much as possible about any conditions the child has and what potential effects they could have on development. Learn as much as you can about development during the middle years of childhood. Don't be afraid to ask other professionals for help and guidance if you have any concerns. As a parent/carer or specialist practitioner it is vital that you liaise with other involved professionals, such as **Occupational Therapists**, **Physiotherapists**, and **Paediatricians** to inform your intervention, avoid contraindications and get the best level of care and support for the child.

Throughout this period your child is still growing and developing so you may need to revisit skills that have been covered before at a more complex level or to compensate for growth.

Remember, not everything can be covered in depth, so use the further reading section to find out more about particular topics.

DEVELOPMENT IN MIDDLE CHILDHOOD

Before your child started school, she spent almost all her time with adults. Her social circle was small, and she may have been effectively the centre of her world. Once at school she has to learn to share the attention of new adults with many other children. She will spend more time away from family and more time in school or engaging in other activities. As she experiences more of the world, her own identity starts to form, and the process contributes substantially to the adult she will become. Even at the earliest age, her experiences, responses and learning, are part of preparing her for adulthood.

Children in this range become more self-aware, begin to better recognise their own and others' emotions and should start negotiating and building relationships with their peers. They begin to compare themselves with others and question differences. At the same time, they are adapting to being in school and coping with the gradual escalation of academic learning. Between the ages of 7 to 12 years the child's thinking becomes much more flexible and logical. The child is able to consider more than one variable at a time, take others' perspectives into consideration, and engage in reversible thinking, as long as it linked to concrete (tangible) objects. They start to see that there can be several possible solutions and outcomes to actions or problems. They still however need "real situations" to help them think conceptually, and they have great difficulty thinking in the abstract.

Over time, she should become increasingly independent. No longer a baby, she will want relationships to reflect her new status. She will pay more attention to friendships and want to be accepted and liked. These friendships tend to be same gender and take on increasing importance, offering support, building mutual confidence and self-esteem, and acting as a sounding board.

At the same time her body is growing, she will be able to climb higher, run faster and will want greater physical challenges. Provide supervised opportunities for controlled risk taking like rock climbing or visiting a trampoline park or let her try some of the more challenging activities in the park. Her desire to belong to something outside the immediate family makes this a great time to investigate scouts or clubs. Over time her coordination and balance should improve. However, she will still need to be as active and physically challenged as possible, in order to maximise her coordination and sensory integration as she grows. Exercise burns off excess energy, strengthens developing muscles, and can help children sleep at night.

Sleep remains incredibly important as growth hormone is released during the night. Seek support if your child struggles with sleep as this can impact on mood and growth.

On average children grow between 2 and 3 inches (5–7 cm) and gain around 7 lb/3 kg a year, bones and muscles broaden and lengthen and particularly after growth spurts youngsters may experience growing pains. Growth spurts can be accompanied by an increase in appetite and food intake. Deciduous – or baby – teeth will start to fall out and be replaced by adult teeth. Boys and girls will have similar body shapes, but once puberty starts, development between male and female starts to diverge.

This book does not look at development beyond puberty. However, as puberty now seems to start quite early in children, it is included in middle childhood rather than adolescence, to help you better prepare your child for all the changes that will take place.

If you have concerns about your child's movement, balance, and core stability, speak to her PE teacher and your **Habilitation Specialist**. If you don't consider the activities suggested above to be appropriate for your child, try and find alternatives that will allow her to develop. This could be something as simple as sitting on a gym ball playing catch, using a wobble board, or perhaps installing a smaller trampoline at home.

A study conducted by UNICEF[1] in 2011, using a cohort of 250 young people aged between 8 and 13 from the UK, Spain, and Sweden found that what children wanted was "time with family and friends, to get out and about without having to spend money, to feel secure about who they are rather than what they own, and to be empowered to develop resilience to pressures to consume." Older children placed greater emphasis on friendship and time alone than young children did. Children and young people with vision impairment are no different from the rest of the population. They too want to go out and about, spend time with family and friends, and have fun.

---

1   UNICEF Children's Wellbeing in UK, Sweden and Spain: the Role of Inequality and Materialism, Ipsos MORI Child Wellbeing Report June 2011

Part 2

1: Personal safety

1.00	Personal safety
1.01	Name
1.02	Home address
1.03	Home phone number
1.04	Family names
1.05	School names and address
1.06	School phone
1.07	Staff names/faces
1.08	What to do if lost
1.09	How to ask for help
1.10	Fire alarm procedure
1.11	"Stranger danger"/safer stranger strategies
1.12	Awareness of danger
1.13	Respond to stop
1.14	Telephones
1.15	Use of home telephone
1.16	How to dial
1.17	999 procedures, 112
1.18	Understanding tones
1.19	Recognition of telephone box
1.20	Use of payphone
1.21	Mobile phone usage – text and call
1.22	Online safety
1.23	Personal profiles
1.24	Apps
1.25	Road safety skills
1.26	Controlled crossings

DOI: 10.4324/9781003280132-4

Activities to work on these skills

Making an emergency call activity

My fire evacuation plan

Emergency

Using a Pelican crossing

iPhone checklist

Prerequisite Skills

Number recognition 0–9

Finger separation

Manual dexterity

Following instructions

Handouts

Emergency service handout

My safety rules

Apps for staying safe

Useful apps for travellers.

Useful websites and books

Emergency

www.scouts.org.uk/activities/emergency-999/

The correct way to make an emergency call, Dorset Fire and Rescue can be watched at the following link or by searching in YouTube for "The Correct Way to Make an Emergency 999 Call from DWFireRescue":

https://www.youtube.com/watch?v=fTb_jCnbutk

BBC cartoon video, calling 999 in an emergency:

www.bbc.co.uk/teach/class-clips-video/pshe-ks2--ks3-how-to-make-an-emergency-call/zg3pxbk

Dealing with an emergency:

www.wmfs.net/safety/emergency/

Identifying risks

ROSPA:

www.rospa.com/resources/information-hubs/keeping-kids-safe

Child Accident Prevention Trust:

www.capt.org.uk/

Safety centres

www.safetycentrealliance.org.uk

Safety Centres equip children and young people with the knowledge they need to make informed life choices, enable them to recognise key risks and dangers, and empower them with the confidence to take actions which will reduce the risks to themselves and others. Centres exist in

Birmingham – Safeside	**Bristol – Lifeskills**	**Cheshire FRS – Safety Central**
Leicester – Warning Zone	**Gloucester – Skillzone**	**Greater Manchester FRS**
North Wales – Dangerpoint	**Milton Keynes – Hazard Alley**	**Newcastle – Safety Works**
London – Sutton Life Centre		**Other SCA Members**

www.360skillsforlife.org/ will be in Dorset, but not up and running at the time of writing.

Road safety

www.roadwise.co.uk/schools/using-the-road/green-cross-code/

www.rospa.com/road-safety/advice/pedestrians/children-road-safety

www.think.gov.uk/education-resources/ road safety education resources by age https:// roadsafety.scot/ https://roadsafety.scot/wp-content/uploads/2019/04/Road-Safety-Step-by -Step-pocket-guide-1.pdf guide for CYP with additional needs

www.childline.org.uk/ stranger danger/safer stranger

Online safety

www.thinkuknow.co.uk/

www.internetmatters.org/

Mental Health and all types of abuse

www.nspcc.org.uk/keeping-children-safe/

Direct support for children and young people on a broad range of topics:

www.childline.org.uk/

PERSONAL SAFETY

This can be quite an emotive topic as it is natural for parents and carers to worry about the risks facing their child. Allowing a child to develop age and stage appropriate independence and keeping that same child safe can feel like a delicate balancing act. The advantage for professionals is they don't have the same emotional ties and can be more rational about what a child can realistically achieve, but they also need to recognise just how hard it can be for a parent to let go.

As children move into middle childhood they start to want to move away from the security of parents and place increasing importance on the opinion and activity of peers. This is a normal part of growing up. They don't want to be perceived as childish and want to do the things that older children do, but it's a challenge. Most children overcome their own anxiety and fear bit by bit and build the level of risk-taking gradually, sometimes encouraged by peers or siblings. Risk-taking in a small familiar group helps children learn self-control as they take turns and work with others and also develop persistence and resilience as they struggle to succeed. These are crucial steps in social development.

Encouraging small risk-taking and gradually allowing increased personal responsibility will help your child learn about calculated risk and appropriate decision-making. The more you teach your child, the safer he will be. Take opportunities as they present themselves, delivering little and often, rather than formal teaching. Every time you cross the road, draw his attention to your decision-making processes, involve him in pressing the button on the pelican crossing, ask him to tell you when the road is clear and you can cross. Alert him to potential risk and offer positive solutions. Each road crossing is a calculated risk, the more practice you have the more accurate the calculation. Elsewhere, start small, for instance, let him go and look at the games in the supermarket, but tell him if he can't find you, not to leave the store, but locate customer services or a member of staff and they'll call you. Build the layers of protection, quietly making them the norm.

1.01–1.09 IDENTITY AND SUPPORTING ADULTS

Rehearse your child's name and address together. Make sure he recognises where he lives as being his address and check he can give his address out clearly in a standardised fashion. Once he starts going out and about independently you may like to create a card in an accessible format that he can carry. This can prove useful in a stressful situation when even basic information can be forgotten. Just the security of having a back-up may boost his confidence. You may also like to use an identifier on the property, a wind chime or garden ornament that reinforces his location as home. If he has some useful vision a distinctive light will also identify the house as the light fails.

He should also know the name of his school as a minimum, and once he progresses to travelling independently, he should also know the address and phone number. If he is going anywhere alone or is allowed to walk at a distance, you should have agreed strategies in place for what to do if things go wrong. This should include where and how to seek help.

If he has a phone he can call you, or another relative or school and explain his predicament. Alternatively, he should seek assistance from agreed sources. Once in school, make sure your child knows where to go for help and support. Schools have different pastoral support systems, but usually he will have a designated mentor or teaching assistant to offer a first line of support, or it may be a class teacher, or in bigger secondary schools a form tutor or Head of Year who will be most approachable. Find out and make sure he knows and is comfortable to take problems to someone in school. As part of transition, some schools prepare booklets and information about the layout of school, the school day, and the names and photographs of staff, particularly those most appropriate to new starters.

Over time, you need to increase the level of independence you give your child. That means allowing him to do things alone. Children always tell you that everybody else is allowed to do whatever it is they want you to allow, but if you speak to other parents, you may find this is not true. However, by the time most children reach top juniors – year 5 or 6, they are wanting to travel to and from school independently or with friends. This experience stands them in good stead when they are looking at the more complex journey that is likely when travelling to secondary school. For children with **SSI** the feasibility of independent home-to- school travel will be dependent on their proximity to school, on the complexity of road crossings between home and school, the child's orientation and mobility skills, and his maturity and cognitive ability. A wealth of preparation will have had to go into this one small step.

In conjunction with your **Habilitation Specialist**, plan how you can gradually increase your child's independence. This will be specific to your child and location but is likely to include strategies like allowing your child to walk from the gates into school alone, and then extending this from the last road crossing, whilst still supporting your child on the more complex elements of the route. It is important to build your child's confidence and independence in as many ways as possible to prepare for this. You can start with simple things like letting your child pay for goods with support, then stepping back and letting him pay independently and progressing to waiting outside the shop. You can also start getting your child to locate a pelican crossing and press the button, before telling you when it's safe to cross, and then progressing to letting him actually make the decision for you both to cross.

1.10–1.13 DEALING WITH DANGER

1.10 FIRE!

A fire in the home is terrible for anyone, but for a child with a vision impairment the fact that he cannot see where the fire is could put him in greater immediate danger. Reduce the risk of him making poor choices by planning and practising evacuation in the event of fire. You can use "My fire evacuation plan" (pages 99–100) to discuss and plan your child's safest escape route. The more you practise, the more likely your child will respond without thinking. If a child doesn't have the knowledge to flee – and that includes secure knowledge of a route – his instinct is to hide. Keep the escape route clear at all times.

Make sure your child is introduced to the sound of your smoke alarm, or fire alarm if you live in shared premises. Use this alarm to trigger specific responses. You may also like to demonstrate the carbon monoxide alarm too if you have one. Many properties have one device that scans for both threats.

At school your child will be expected to practise fire drills fairly regularly. There are also drills to practise for other scenarios, but all these need to be explained to the CYPVI beforehand. The school should warn the student before the first practice and he should be told beforehand what to expect. Every school must have a fire evacuation plan and if your child needs specific assistance or procedures put in place, he may need a Personal Emergency Evacuation Plan (PEEP). This will outline clearly what he should do, what support he needs to safely exit the building and who will provide it. This plan should never include expecting a child to wait anywhere alone. As well as seeking advice from the Fire Service, the school may also like to seek advice from the **Habilitation Specialist** who will familiarise your child with the building and develop routes.

1.11 THREATS FROM PEOPLE

As you start allowing your child more freedom and independence your anxiety levels will rise. It is hard letting your child go. However, there is much you can do to prepare your child for independence. The more he knows, the better his understanding of the world and the people in it, the safer he will be. As parents we fear abduction or attacks on our children, but these are very rare. Children are more at risk from their own ill-considered actions, not applying basic road safety, accepting challenges and dares, careless online safety, and a lack of understanding of their own mortality.

Teach your child these basic safety rules to use whenever they feel under threat and prepare him for a variety of scenarios. So, for instance, if you are ever not at school to collect him, he stays in school unless the person collecting has been authorised by you and knows the password or code.

There is a separate handout of "My safety rules" (pages 137–138) in the appendices.

Safety rules

- Stay away from strangers. Explain what makes a person a stranger. Note that even someone with a familiar face is a stranger if you do not know him or her well. Make sure your child has an understanding of safer strangers, e.g. someone in an appropriate uniform, police, paramedic, or a woman with a small child or a buggy
- Stay away from anyone who is following you on foot or in a car. Don't get close to them or feel as though you must answer any questions they ask you
- Run and scream if someone tries to force you to go somewhere with them or tries to push you into a car
- If you can get away, and can see the car, run in the direction opposite to the way the car is facing. The vehicle would have to turn round to come after you, giving you a bit more time
- Set up a secret code word. Tell your child not to go with anyone under any circumstances unless that person also knows this code word
- Agree a coded message for your child to text you or call when out with friends or at a sleepover that will mean, "Pick me up I don't feel comfortable". Ring back with an excuse they can use to leave
- Adults shouldn't ask children for help. For example, a child shouldn't trust grown-ups who ask for directions or for help finding a puppy or kitten. A child who is approached in this way should tell the person, "Wait here and I'll check with my Mum or Dad", and then find his or her parents right away
- Ask for help when you are lost, stay still, don't just wander. If you get lost in a public place, immediately ask someone who works there for help
- Always ask for permission before going anywhere with anybody. Ask a parent or the grown-up in charge before leaving home or the play area, or before going into someone else's home. Do not accept **any** unplanned offers for a ride – from someone known or unknown
- Always tell a parent or carer where you are going, how you will get there, who is going with you, and when you will be back. Be home at the agreed time or ensure you let your family know

1.12–1.13 OTHER RISKS

Before letting your child go further abroad or travel even semi-independently from you, ensure that he will always respond to "STOP". You need to be sure that in an emergency he will actually respond to warnings from yourself or others. This is particularly important if bystanders can see a risk that he cannot.

The most obvious risks out and about are from traffic and deep water, but children with vision impairments need to be protected from risks in the home too. Clutter around the home or school can cause falls and a lack of safety procedures can result in burns and scalds. Burns and scalds are covered in more detail in the handout (pages 147–148). In the garden make sure that all gardening implements are away safely and that trampolines are fitted with a safety net. If you have a pond, make sure that something clearly warns the child that the pond is there, like a change of surface from grass to gravel, or fence it off until your child is older. If you are not sure about potential risks, take a look at the RoSPA pages on keeping kids safe www.rospa .com/resources/information-hubs/keeping-kids-safe or the Child Accident Prevention Trust, www .capt.org.uk/. If you can get your child to one of the Safety Centres, located in some areas of the country, these equip children and young people with the knowledge they need to make informed life choices, enable them to recognise key risks and dangers, and empower them with the confidence to take actions which will reduce the risks to themselves and others, all whilst in a safe environment. These are often not accessible to individual families, but school, scouts, or your local RNIB branch, or society for vision impaired people, for example, may be able to organise a trip.

1.14–1.21 TELEPHONES

It is helpful to teach even younger children what to do in an emergency. The easiest way to access emergency help is via the telephone. Your child will need to know how to dial the emergency

> **In an Emergency call**
> **999 or 112**

services, and what will happen. Successful dialling on most phones needs the ability to recognise and sequence numbers, but also the correct number to dial. Children watch a great deal of American films and television programmes, as a result a surprising number believe 911 to be the emergency number in the UK. Emergency calls are free and available 24 hours a day from any phone.

Payphones: Although becoming more rare on the high street, ensure your child is aware of the existence of public telephone boxes or payphones, can recognise one, and understands how they can be used. They can be investigated on mobility lessons, or at any point when out and about together. Practise opening the door from both sides, locating the phone, dialling a number, and inserting money or a card. Ensure the child is aware that dialling 100 secures operator assistance, including making reverse charge calls.

Landlines: Not everyone has landlines, but it is always better, where possible, to call the emergency services from a landline rather than a mobile phone, as a landline provides a geographical area code and can be traced more easily. They can also be easier for a young child with little or no vision to use independently

In the days of rotary (dial) telephones, 999 was selected for best accessibility reasons, because in the dark or in dense smoke 999 could be dialled by placing a finger one hole away from the dial stop and rotating the dial to the full extent three times. This made it easier for everyone, including those with vision impairment to dial the emergency number. The **9** is less easy to locate on a modern push-button phone, but has the advantage of repetition, so the finger does not need to move.

112 came from the EU. It has the advantage of working across Europe and the **1** and **2** are easy to locate as the first and second buttons at the top of the phone. Push-button phones, both landlines and mobile, have a tactile dot on the number 5 to help with number recognition.

When you call, a BT operator will ask which service you need – fire, police or ambulance. If your child is not sure the operator will try to help by asking questions. Your child will need to know the address where they need assistance and be able to give a basic outline of the problem. There are links to several videos in "Useful websites and books" for this section, which you can play through with your child to rehearse emergency calls as well as using the activities provided. The emergency service handout on pages 134–136 includes a phone template to reinforce learning.

Make sure your child can recognise the dialling tone, as well as the ring, engaged, and unobtainable tones. Save useful information and phone numbers of family members or other sources of help in a format your child can access and keep it in an agreed place. Teach your child never to share personal information with an unknown caller.

Mobile phones: When does your child need a mobile? Obviously, this is completely down to parental choice, but once he starts going out and about independently, he is safer with a phone. Your old phone is the best choice for a younger child. Apple remains the market leader for access with vision impairment, but you really don't need a state-of-the-art one. In fact, carrying a high-end phone can make your child a target. An older device offers all the same functions and often has the advantage of retaining a home button, which simplifies use of the phone.

You can support your child learning to use his phone. Apple provides extensive accessibility information online, including guidance on VoiceOver gestures and there is also an iPhone checklist on pages 104–105.

Whilst your child does not need data in order to make phone calls, he will need credit and sufficient charge in his phone. It is also a good idea to save a range of basic numbers into his phone, including school and family members. Lay down clear guidelines about exactly what the phone can be used for and when. If you allow your child to have data on the phone, there are a number of apps that will help keep him safer when out and about. However, access to data brings its own risks that are outlined below. New apps are developed all the time and outdated ones drop out of use. The list of "Apps for staying safe" on page 139 was correct at the time of publication.

If your child needs to call emergency services from a mobile, they do not need credit, the phone does not need to be unlocked and even if they have no, or a weak signal from their service provider, an emergency call will attempt to connect to another network. However, you will be unable to receive a call on that network, even if the inbound call is from emergency services.

Don't forget to use the ICE (In Case of Emergency) app or facility on the phone which lets you put your emergency information on your lock screen so that anyone can access it if need be. As well as displaying an emergency contact, it allows you to save information about your child's medical conditions, medication, or allergies.

The Silent Solution: In the event of an intruder in the house or fear of domestic violence, your child may want to ring the emergency services, but not feel able to speak in case he is heard. If you call 999 and don't speak, the BT operator will listen for background noises (shouting, coughs, noises, taps on the phone and will hang on the line for a certain period of time. If they believe you need help but can't speak, the call will be transferred to the police first. Then you will hear an automated police message that begins with "you are through to the police". It will ask you to press 55 to be put through to police call management. Stay on the line, this way you are indicating to the police that you may have an emergency that keeps you from talking, and they will do everything they can to determine your location so they can deploy officers to you. The phone buttons can be pressed to respond to questions so the police can gather as much information as possible. **This only works on mobile phones**. If you are silent on a landline, they will endeavour to track the call and offer reassurance, but there is no two-way communication without speaking.

1.22 ONLINE SAFETY

There is a range of apps to use on mobiles to keep safe both for general safety and for navigation. These can be found, together with their uses in the appendices on pages 139 and 140. Remember apps change constantly, so although accurate at the time of publication, support can cease at any time.

There are many unscrupulous people waiting to prey on the unsuspecting and vulnerable, so teach your child to be wary. Show them how to restrict their profile so that only friends can see their posts and communicate with them. Watch online activity as far as possible and use parental controls on all devices. Choose usernames that are not easily identifiable and advise them not to share any personal data over social media. Children can be nasty to one another at any time, but somehow the distance and anonymity of online messaging makes it seem less personal to the perpetrator and things can quickly escalate.

The Thinkuknow websites for advice about staying safe when on a phone, tablet, or computer are helpful to professionals, parents and children alike. There are separate pages for children and young people aged 4–7, 8—10, 11–13, and 14 plus.

1.25–1.26 ROAD SAFETY

Your child needs to develop more advanced road safety skills before moving on to genuine independent travel. This means developing not only an understanding of controlled crossings, like zebra and pelican crossings, but also uncontrolled crossings. Sighted children are not able to judge speed and distance until around the age of 10, so speed and distance calculations are likely to be much more difficult if your child is relying on limited or no vision and hearing.

Pelican, puffin, and toucan crossings are the easiest to use safely because they provide a clear indicator of when to cross, either through the beeps, using the red and green man, the tactile indicator under the control box or by watching the WAIT sign go out. Build routes to use these types of crossings, or bridges and underpasses as far as possible.

Zebra crossings require more complex decision-making that may need rehearsing. CYPVI should not cross just because they feel pressured when one vehicle stops, or if someone beeps or flashes at them. None of these are clear indicators that it is safe to cross. If your child uses a cane, either a symbol cane or a long cane, encourage him to use it when crossing roads, even if he doesn't use it anywhere else. This should make drivers more tolerant of the decision-making process. If your child is not sure, or feels pressured – step away from the crossing and wait for a new opportunity.

On uncontrolled crossings, unless it is a very minor road or drive with little or no traffic, young people should be encouraged to *indent* – i.e., walk down the side road further way from the junction, before crossing and returning to the main road they were travelling along. This reduces the number of different directions traffic can be travelling, which can be difficult to distinguish with reduced vision or when dependent on hearing alone. It also allows the driver and the pedestrian more reaction time and makes the pedestrian more confident that when lining up with the kerb, a straight crossing will take him to the opposite pavement and not out into the junction. If the CYPVI has enough vision, he should select a crossing point that allows him and drivers maximum vision. If you find blister paving and dropped kerbs at a junction, that is usually the least safe place to cross.

Work together with your **Habilitation Specialist** to plan safe routes for your child. This may sometimes mean travelling a little further in order to use a controlled crossing point.

Find out more about general road safety teaching from RoSPA –

www.rospa.com/road-safety/advice/pedestrians/children-road-safety or the Think website www.think.gov.uk/education-resources/. If your child has additional needs the Step-by-Step Guide produced by Road Safety Scotland is beautifully clear, https://roadsafety.scot/wp-content/uploads/2019/04/Road-Safety-Step-by-Step-pocket-guide-1.pdf.

2: Advanced dressing and fastenings

2.00	Advanced dressing and fastenings
2.01	Small buttons
2.02	Zip, open-ended
2.03	Buckle
2.04	Bows and shoelaces
2.05	Tights
2.06	Necktie
2.07	Hook and eye – or trouser/bra fastener
2.08	Bags, belts, braces
2.09	Clasp (as on purse)
2.10	Put watch on/off
2.11	Jewellery on/off
2.12	Locker
2.13	Bolt
2.14	Door chain
2.15	Key in lock
2.16	Toilet lock
2.17	Turning taps on and off

DOI: 10.4324/9781003280132-5

TO WORK ON THESE SKILLS

Prerequisite skills

Hand strength, finger separation, manual dexterity

Handouts

Tying bows and laces

Open-ended zipper

Tying a necktie

Tactile marking and labelling

Websites and books

In YouTube, search for: How to tie a tie – 3 simple necktie knots easy to tie:

https://youtu.be/jKYTVxoaMQA

Necktie four in hand: In YouTube, search for: Easily tie four-in-hand necktie knot:

https://youtu.be/wObObp6IoaU

Whilst there is more tolerance in primary schools, even here there is an expectation that children can put their own coats on to go outside and get dressed and undressed for PE without excessive help. If your child needs help, it makes them feel different, and this impacts on confidence and self-esteem. Once children and young people get to secondary school – particularly in mainstream, there is an expectation that they will not only be able to successfully dress themselves, but that they will do so in a reasonable space of time. Working on this beforehand will build their confidence, speed up the task, and ensure your child is not adult-dependent and thereby marginalised in the group.

2.01–2.07 ADVANCED DRESSING SKILLS

If your child attends school, the chances are she will be expected to wear a uniform. The uniform style will largely dictate the skills that your child will have to master, but there are sometimes workarounds, provided your school does not insist on all items bearing the school badge or logo. A number of retailers, including George, Next and Marks and Spencer produce a range of adaptive clothing, including uniforms that offer elasticated waists and concealed Velcro® that are largely indistinguishable from the standard range. You may need to plan and order these in advance online, rather than finding them in store. Marks and Spencer offers the range through to age 18.

These types of clothing can be helpful if your child struggles with hooks and eyes and the trouser bar, so often used on school trousers. Trousers tend to have elasticated waists for younger children, but then older boys' trousers often swap to a hook and bar. Practise with the trousers off, when there is no need to stretch and overlap the material the same way, before trying to fasten them when worn.

Hooks and eyes are also a problem on bras. Fastening a bra behind your back can be quite a struggle. There is no reason it can't be fastened at the front and swung round, but the fastening itself can be an issue. There are many different sports or pull-on bras on the market that may be a suitable alternative whilst learning to master the fastening. Buy a large hook and eye – the bigger the better – and fasten it to two pieces of material to learn the principles of how to fasten them together. Progress to replacing the fastenings on an old bra with a single, larger hook and eye to explain the way the bra fastens when on. Get the feel for positioning the bra correctly and stretching the elastic. Remember the motion is very different when fastening in front than from behind. Finally, move on to the real bra fastening. Make sure your child is confident before going out and about. There are often multiple hooks and multiple rows of eyes. If you only hook one on, movements can cause stress and it may ping out. This can be extremely embarrassing and is not easy to rectify if the child can't adjust the fastening from behind her back.

If your child still struggles with sliding the zip locator pin into the retainer box on open-ended zips, opt for a coat that has an extra fastening layer, like buttons or Velcro® so she is not dependent on someone else to fasten her coat. Practise with bigger zips so it is easier to feel how it slots together. Use the "Open-ended zipper" handout on pages 145–146 to ensure you use consistent terminology when describing the zip. If your child has useful vision, buy two zips of contrasting colours and mix and match so the locator pin sliding into the retainer box is more visible. Keep working on the full range of fastenings so your child has the maximum choice of clothing.

Buttons: As buttons get smaller, they require more dexterity. In some cases, if the buttonhole is tight, you can change the button for a smaller one, so it goes through more easily. Colour contrast the button and material for practice.

Buckles on shoes are quite difficult to master because of the size and the awkwardness of reaching down. Start with buckles on belts or on wider bag straps, before moving on to shoes. Practise with shoes off before attempting with them on. If your child has some useful vision, use a buckle that contrasts with the belt or strap, and the bigger the better to begin.

BOWS AND LACES

Tying laces is definitely not an easy skill to learn, or to teach. See the "Bows and laces" handout on pages 142–144 for additional tricks and tips on teaching bows and laces.

Children who have a vision impairment may have problems with coordinating the connection between what their eyes are seeing and what their hands are doing — essentially, eye–hand coordination. They become easily confused by all of the criss-crossing and looping of laces, and their visual system suddenly cannot distinguish one lace from the other, which is why different coloured or textured laces may help. Regular practice really does help. Remember bows are not just needed for shoelaces, so it is worth persisting with bows to build confidence and reduce dependence on staff and family members.

At secondary school your child will probably be expected to wear aprons for certain technology lessons. Technology subjects may vary from school to school, but may include food technology, design and technology – resistant materials, textiles, and graphics. Some schools provide aprons, others expect pupils to have their own.

Aprons do not have to be tied at the back. Cross the strings behind the back and fasten at the front if it is easier.

Practise at home with ribbons tied round a leg, before moving on to aprons.

You can knot two different coloured or textured ribbons together to help your child differentiate between the different strands and can use wired ribbon to help keep the loops in position.

Many secondary schools also require more formal school shoes and without the ability to tie laces the choice is limited. Learn the principle of tying bows first, before attempting laces when the shoe is on the foot.

Tights often get in a twist and become very uncomfortable. When learning how to put tights on, start with leggings first to practise keeping everything lined up. Then move onto tights, but select a larger size to start, as they allow more leg and foot movement and use cotton or woollen tights rather than nylon. Show her where the gusset and the toe are and demonstrate how to scrunch each leg up into a manageable size before inserting the foot. Sheer nylon tights or pantyhose have rather fallen out of fashion, and they both cling and stretch and catch as you pull them on, they also snag and run easily making the task that much harder. If tights are still a problem, most schools now accept trousers as an alternative to skirts and tights.

Work out your own systems at home so your child knows where to find her uniform, or appropriate clothing for the day. That could be on a chair or on top of a chest of drawers. Once she has mastered the dressing skills, then you can consider progressing to her selecting appropriate clothes for herself. Teach her to return clothes to the chair the right way round, so she could put them on again if desired, or give her a designated dirty washing basket. Check she can hang clothes securely on a peg for PE lessons. Some schools use lockers too, so teach her how to fold clothing so it is wearable afterwards. See "Household chores" on pages 186–188 to find out more about teaching folding.

Many secondary schools still have a necktie as part of the school uniform. There may be an elasticated or clip-on version, but not always and it's not a bad idea to learn how to tie a necktie. It can be a useful skill when it comes to interviews in the future. The four-in-hand or half Windsor are the easiest knots to tie. The handout on neckties gives more details on how to teach your child, and the videos mentioned above demonstrate the techniques clearly.

Children spend much of their educational years in uniform. Uniform is deliberately the same for each child to engender a sense of belonging and reduce bullying. However, this means that every item of clothing looks identical and identifying clothing in the mad scramble to get dressed again after PE can be difficult. There is a "Tactile marking and labelling" handout with more details on how to label clothing on pages 149–150.

Matching clothes: As your child gets older, she may want to start selecting her own clothes. There are several different methods that you can use to identify clothing. Drawers can be labelled, and clothing separated into colours and types.

Some people like to seek the help of a reliable sighted friend to create matching outfits or ensembles, which that then be put away or hung together in the wardrobe ready for use.

Others prefer to identify individual items of clothing by touch or use a Penfriend device to confirm which it is. Those who are more app orientated can use Seeing AI to identify the colours or BeMyEyes to get an online volunteer to check for clashes. More care needs to be taken with BeMyEyes and other services that offer human support.

2.08 SMALL CLASPS AND BUCKLES

Watches can be difficult to fasten and may be becoming less fashionable with teens who tend to look at phones, but most schools don't allow mobiles to be accessed during the school day, so a watch provides a useful alternative.

Talking watches/tactile watches often fasten with a buckle or flip over clasp. These are small fastenings that require dexterity. Watches and jewellery have to be taken off for PE but fastening a buckle one handed when you cannot see requires a great deal of practice.

Begin with a larger buckle, like that on a belt that can be explored easily, and two hands can be used to fasten. Gradually reduce the buckle size, until the child can fasten a watch-sized buckle when off the wrist. You may need to describe the process in detail. Once you have mastered this off the wrist, move on to fastening and unfastening the watch on the wrist.

To wear a watch on the left hand: Teach your child to put their watch down flat on the wrist, with the winder towards the hand. Hold the watch in place and put the arm down on a flat surface then, with the buckle on the surface and the other end of the strap hanging over, the child can feed the strap into the buckle with the right hand.

Mirror the process to wear on the right hand.

You may like to consider swapping to a Velcro® strap if your child cannot get the hang of the buckle.

If you allow your child to go into school wearing jewellery – remember that the school may require it to be removed. Pierced earrings are particularly difficult to remove and insert without considerable practice.

2.12–2.16 LOCKS

There are so many different types of locks and the techniques for each vary enormously. Secondary schools often use lockers to store coats and equipment throughout the day. Suggest your child is provided with a locker at the end of the row, with easy access and with a lock set at a comfortable height to use. The keys and the locks are often small and fiddly, so consider using a key extender to make it easier and keep the key on a larger keyring to make it easier to find in a bag. Ensure there is something tactile, or otherwise recognisable, on the outside of the locker, so you child can be sure it is the correct locker they are opening. If the key is inserted into the wrong locker it may jam.

Show your child each different lock you encounter to build her understanding. You can also see if you can borrow a manipulation board, or even make one yourself for your child to practise on. Melissa and Doug™ do some lovely small durable ones that are not too childish.

It is important to be able to manipulate a variety of locks, because once behind a locked door it is easy to fall prey to panic and become trapped. Practice builds confidence and reduces the fear. This can be a particular problem in toilets where there are no standard lock styles or fastenings.

If your child has a front door key and carries other keys on a keyring, add a key cover to be sure they can identify the right key. You can also get extenders to make it easier to hold and insert in the lock if a child finds it difficult. If your child gets home school transport and has an escort in the vehicle, the Local Authority may require an adult to be at home to receive your child. You may need to negotiate to get permission for your child let herself in independently.

2.17 TAPS

If construction guidance is followed, you would always find the cold tap on the right and hot on the left, but there are always exceptions to every rule! At home you can use an elastic band or a pipe cleaner to reinforce which is hot and which is cold and sometimes you can feel residual warmth, without running the tap.

Try and demonstrate a variety of different tap types. They range from twist on and off, to levers and push down or across and some even have sensors to turn on when hands are placed underneath. Some taps need a considerable amount of force. Using taps is revisited in Section 8.

3: Puberty and personal hygiene

3.00	**Puberty and personal hygiene**
3.01	Locate toilets
3.02	Location of toilet stall and toilet
3.03	Use of toilet stall and toilet
3.04	Location of urinal if appropriate
3.05	Use of urinal
3.06	Location of washbasins
3.07	Handwashing
3.08	Identify hot and cold taps
3.09	Appropriate use of soap or dispenser
3.10	Locate hand drier
3.11	Locate paper towels and bin
3.12	Awareness of puberty
3.13	Understanding of periods
3.14	Sanitary protection awareness
3.15	Use of
3.16	Disposal of
3.17	Wash face
3.18	Washing body
3.19	Haircare – brush
3.20	Haircare – comb
3.21	Clip/bobbles/Alice band
3.22	Hair washing
3.23	Hair drying
3.24	Independent bathing or showering
3.25	Cleaning teeth
3.26	Spots, cleansing, and toning
3.27	Use of appropriate personal care products (including deodorant, makeup, etc., if age appropriate)

Activities to work on these skills

How to wash your hair.

Personal hygiene: daily washing

Activity: My Lego® teeth

Handouts

Toileting issues

Supporting your child with hair washing.

Haircare: Brushing

Personal hygiene, products, tips, and tricks

Facts about periods – teaching guidance

Facts about periods – student handout

The puberty pack

Websites and books

Help your kids with growing up, Robert Winston

What's Happening to me? (Girls' Edition), Susan Meredith 2006, Usborne Books

What's Happening to me? (Boys' Edition), Alex Frith 2013, Usborne Books

From Armpits to Zits: The Book of Yucky Body Bits

Author: Paul Mason | 28 Apr 2011

Growing Up Great! – The Ultimate Puberty Book for Boys

Author: Scott Todnem

Living with a Willy – the inside story Author: Nick Fisher

Celebrate Your Body (And Its Changes, Too) – A Body-Positive Guide for Girls 8+

Author: Sonya Renee Taylor

Celebrate Your Body 2 – The Ultimate Puberty Book for Preteen and Teen Girls

Author: Dr Carrie Leff, Dr Lisa Klein

The Great British Public Toilet Map indicates where public toilets can be found:

www.toiletmap.org.uk/

Changing Places – accessible toilets for those with more complex needs:

www.changing-places.org/find

www.independent.co.uk/extras/indybest/kids/best-kids-hair-brush-b1813960.html

www.rnibbookshare.org/ RNIB Bookshare downloadable accessible books and tactile diagrams

Period pants

www.shethinx.com

www.wuka.co.uk

www.modibodi.co.uk/

So many things change during the period covered by this book. The transition from childhood to adolescence starts, which can be a painful, confusing time for many young people, but it can be even more challenging for those with vision impairment. You will need to tread a fine line as their guide through this maze, sharing information, acting as a confidant and moral compass, and do it all without cramping their style.

At this point in time, they want to look good and be valued by their peers. The approval of friends becomes more important than the approbation of adults. This is even before the onset of any sexual interest and the desire to appeal to others in this way. The right appearance and conforming to perceived norms will suddenly come to the fore. According to children in this phase, the adults know nothing and cannot possibly understand. The idea that their parents might have lived through, and still recall similar emotional traumas is laughable to them.

Without vision, these youngsters may not be as aware of the changes going on with their peers, so their own physical changes may cause surprise and anxiety. This is then compounded by the emotional turbulence some may feel coping with changes out of their control. The changes in neurological function outlined below can cause increased irritability and risk taking, but also bring a greater capacity for abstract thought and problem solving.

Many preadolescent or early adolescent children develop an increased percentage of body fat, in preparation for the adolescent growth spurt. This is entirely normal, but when youngsters are starting to focus on their physical appearance, it can have an adverse effect on body image. Body image is nothing to do with how a young person looks, but everything about how they feel. Growth spurts tend to start in girls between the ages of 9 and 11 (typically 2 years before the onset of menstruation) and in boys it may not start until around 12. Remember that a high proportion of CYPVI also have other conditions that may affect growth and the onset of puberty. Every child is different. Make sure your child is aware of what is going to happen beforehand, and they understand that the changes occur at different times and rates in different individuals.

Young people may also experience a temporary decline in coordination due to sudden growth spurts. During puberty children's growth starts from the extremities in, so the hands and feet grow first, followed by the limbs, and finally, the torso and spine. In times of big growth spurts the part of the brain that deals with spatial awareness can take time to adjust to the new size and shape, resulting in a spell of gangly awkwardness. Vision and perception are also affected because everything is viewed from a higher trajectory, and in some cases certain eye conditions may mean that the ground is not visible in the same way. This is a turning point for a number of youngsters who start to move away from physical exercise, either because they don't enjoy it, because they feel self-conscious, or they are frustrated about the impact of the physical changes. If you factor in the fact that some schools don't understand how to make PE accessible and others actively discourage CYPVI from taking part, non-participation becomes the norm. This is counter intuitive in a period of rapid physical growth and brain development. Activities undertaken now set the mind and skillsets for the future.

The onset of puberty, particularly in girls, seems to have changed and many girls are experiencing it much younger than they were even a couple of generations ago. Scientists are aware and investigations are ongoing, but as yet the cause is unknown. Although the average age is higher, some girls can start their periods as early as 8 or 9. This means that it is really important that you have conversations about the onset of menstruation early, and preferably before it happens. Depending on the age and maturity of the child, you may prefer to be selective about what you tell them, but stick to the truth and with younger children, use it sparingly. If they want to know more, they will ask. However, you will then have to return to the topic at a later date to fill in the gaps.

THE BRAIN

Not only will your child have to contend with physical change, but at the same time the brain is rewiring itself, and this will impact on the way the child will think and act as they mature. It was originally believed that the human brain was formed in early childhood, however MRI scans taken throughout childhood and into adolescence and young adulthood, show the radical changes that occur in adolescence.

Approaching adolescence, the brain begins over-producing grey matter. This is a wonderful time for children to take on new experiences and challenges that create new connections in the brain, as the possibilities for development are endless. The feats of learning and the challenges undertaken during this time shape the wiring of the adult brain. Children need to challenge themselves and take risks to promote this growth. These strengthened neural connections endure a lifetime, but those connections that are no longer used will be pruned or eliminated. Pruning permits the brain to organise and speed up its circuitry and refine the thinking processes.

Neuroscientists at the American National Institute of Mental Health (www.nimh.nih.gov) have been able to show that the pruning starts at the back of the brain and moves forward during adolescence.[1] The parts of the brain that control sensory and motor skills mature first, becoming more specialised and efficient. The prefrontal cortex matures last. This is the area responsible for language, impulse control, abstract thinking, and decision-making. Until it is developed, decisions are based more on the amygdala, the centre of the fight or flight response which can explain the overly emotional and impulsive responses you might see in your child.

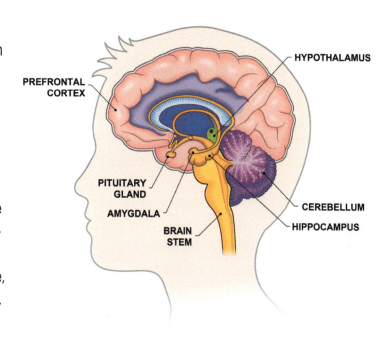

3.01–3.11 TOILETING AND HAND WASHING

TOILETS AND BATHROOMS IN FAMILIAR SETTINGS

At home or school your child should be familiar with both the layout and usage of the amenities. Procedures that were introduced from an early age, like washing hands after using the toilet should all still be employed.

At home, your child should be able to locate the bathroom and use the toilet independently. If not, speak to your **Habilitation Specialist** to see what support can be offered. You may also like to refer back to some of the strategies offered in *Supporting Life Skills for Young Children*, or if you think there are physical or sensory issues, take a look at the "Toileting issues" handout on pages 151–153. The bathroom is easily identifiable in terms of echo location because of the

---

1   https://health.usnews.com/health-news/family-health/brain-and-behavior/articles/2008/11/26/how-to-deploy-the-amazing-power-of-the-teen-brain accessed 11 October 2021

usual absence of soft furnishings, and it is normally small enough to learn the layout quickly by trailing. Keep all items like toilet paper, wipes, soap, and towels in a set location and encourage your child to return them correctly after use.

If your child has useful vision, try and use contrast to make navigation and use easier. If your preferred product merges with the background, consider using a different coloured dispenser or dish. If the bathroom is predominantly white, consider putting blue loo flush in the cistern to help pick out the toilet bowl, consider maybe a contrasting toilet seat or perhaps add a pedestal mat to help locate the toilet.

At school your child should be accompanied to the toilets if they need extra support. As they mature however, they may wish to start using the toilet alone. The school, together with the **Habilitation Specialist** should ensure that your child can navigate to and move around the toilet space safely if at all possible. Sometimes when your child moves class, this may necessitate them using different toilets, so re-familiarisation may be necessary.

Ideally splashbacks should contrast with the washbasin, and toilet doors should contrast both with the flooring and the cubicle frame. Usually in schools, soap is in fixed locations on the wall, just over the washbasin. Warm air hand driers and paper towel dispensers are also fixed on the wall. Bins do often move, so ensure the difference between paper and sanitary bins is made clear.

If your child moves up to secondary school, accessing toilets may again become a problem. In addition to familiarisation with the route and the layout, there can be some additional problems in newer builds. In an attempt to stamp out bullying some schools have opted for open-plan toilet areas. This can mean that as the students come out of the cubicle, there is no buffer zone to allow for adjustments and dress hiccoughs to be pointed out by others, like the need to untuck skirts from knickers, or ditch the toilet roll stuck to your shoes. In this design you often find there is nothing to distinguish the male and female pupil toilet areas, so some low vision students worry they might use the wrong ones. Some students just accept it, but others find it terribly uncomfortable and anxiety inducing. If your child finds this set-up difficult you can request that additional signage and markers are put up or that they are allowed to use the disabled toilets.

TOILETS AND BATHROOMS OUT AND ABOUT

Suddenly, access to toilets and bathrooms becomes more problematic. Public toilets are a particular issue – can they go in with you still? Do they want to? Or would they like a bit more privacy?

Tricks and tips for toilets out and about.

✓ Get a **RADAR** key if you haven't already. This gives your child access to disabled toilets out and about. The very fact that a key is required means that the facilities are usually cleaner. You should be able to obtain a RADAR key by contacting the Access Officer at your local authority. For those who can't get a RADAR key from your local authority, you can obtain one from RADAR directly for a small charge, by calling or emailing them. They are also available on Amazon. You then have the option of staying outside or going in with your child, depending on their preference

✓ If there is no disabled toilet, consider the parent and baby changing facilities

✓ The Great British Public Toilet Map (www.toiletmap.org.uk) indicates where you can find public toilets and indicates disabled facilities. Remember too, that most larger supermarkets and department stores, shopping centres, and travel hubs like train and bus stations provide toilet facilities. Those in stations are often chargeable, so your child will need to be able to deal with that too

✓ Urinal use is optional, particularly if you can't see enough to locate them. Everyone can use cubicles if they prefer

✓ Standard accessible toilets do not meet the needs of all people with a disability; if your child has more complex needs look for Changing Places. The link allows you to find the nearest changing places facilities to your location. Access is again via a RADAR key. www.changing-places.org/find

✓ Equip your child with a small pack of toilet wipes or tissues in case the toilet paper is not easily locatable or has run out. A small hand sanitiser can also be helpful

✓ Many new buildings and places like colleges, universities, and hospitals have gender neutral toilets. These are individual toilet rooms, rather than cubicles, so make sure your child has been introduced to the concept

✓ If you child is choosing to go into toilets alone, make sure that they can lock and unlock a wide variety of fastenings. Disabled toilets often have a large latch that drops over, but many toilet cubicles have variations of bolts or locking knobs. Unlocking a stiff lock can sometime be panic inducing – so practise with a wide range

3.12 PHYSICAL CHANGES IN PUBERTY

If you are going to be talking to your child about puberty, it is helpful to understand the timeline and the physical changes that take place. Be factual and use the correct terminology. If your child is a confident reader and you feel that the conversation may be too embarrassing, you may like to introduce the topic through one of the books listed at the start of this section, otherwise – read on!

In both males and females, puberty begins when the hypothalamus in the brain produces gonadotropin-releasing hormone (GnRH), which signals to the body it's ready to start developing into an adult. This then triggers a wide range of changes that take place over several years.

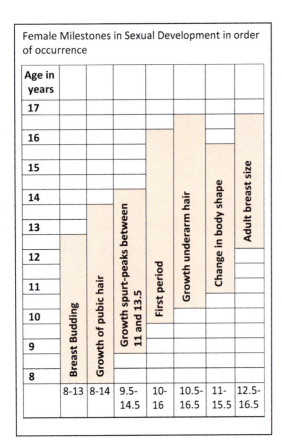

Female Milestones in Sexual Development in order of occurrence. Age in years chart (8–17) showing: Breast Budding (8-13), Growth of pubic hair (8-14), Growth spurt-peaks between 11 and 13.5 (9.5-14.5), First period (10-16), Growth underarm hair (10.5-16.5), Change in body shape (11-15.5), Adult breast size (12.5-16.5).

During puberty, sexual development occurs in a set sequence. However, when the changes start and how rapidly they progress varies from person to person. For girls, puberty begins somewhere between 8 and 10 years and lasts about 4 years. Boys usually begin puberty from 10 onwards and can continue longer. The charts show the typical sequence and normal range of development for the milestones of sexual development.

Both sexes also have hair on their arms and legs that becomes more noticeable in puberty.

In girls, skeletal growth ceases between 16 and 17, in boys it can continue to 20. Between the ages of 12 and 15 boys grow at a rate of 7–9 cm a year.

Everyone's larynx grows during puberty, but a girl's larynx doesn't grow as much as a boy's does. It usually occurs between 14 and 15, but occasionally can be earlier. Voices usually break around 15, but again this is an average. It can be embarrassing and a little worrying when the voice wavers between high and low pitches if you are not aware what is happening.

Involuntary nocturnal emissions of seminal fluid – more commonly known as wet dreams – begin from around 12, but at this point no mature sperm are produced. Masturbation may also begin from around this point. Whilst you may feel uncomfortable talking about masturbation, it is important that CYPVI are reminded that there is a time and place for everything and in terms of masturbation, that place is probably in the bedroom. Young people with no vision can forget that others can see what they are doing, and this can lead to some awkward situations. Equally embarrassing can be spontaneous erections, which can become more frequent during puberty.

Male Milestones in Sexual Development in order of occurrence. Age in years chart (10–18) showing: Growth of scrotum and testes (10.5-17), Change in voice (10.5-18), Lengthening of penis (11-15), Growth of pubic hair (11-14), Growth spurt-peaks 12-15 (12-17), Change of body shape (12-17), Growth of facial and underfund hair (12-18).

Sleep is another factor that impacts as the brain and body are in overdrive during puberty. Preteens and adolescents need between 9 and 11 hours of sleep each night for healthy development. Unfortunately, melatonin, the hormone that encourages sleep is not released at the usual pre bedtime, but instead is released two or three hours later in the night, creating sleep-deprived irritable young people, who want to stay awake all night and sleep all day. This is not down to laziness but is a direct result of the disruption to the circadian rhythm.

There are downloadable diagrams on RNIB Bookshare to help explain human anatomy.

3.13–3.16 PERIODS

Both boys and girls need to know about periods, although not necessarily in the same detail. Teaching about periods is covered in detail in the two "Periods guidance" handouts, one for young people and the other for those supporting them. Here you will find a range of practical solutions and suggestions to address the difficulties faced by CYPVI experiencing periods.

3.17–3.18 PERSONAL CARE

Whilst a grubby face and a gap-toothed grin is cute in a toddler it has the opposite effect in pre-teens and teens, so it is important that proper care is taken. During puberty the body produces more sweat and smells. Sweat is odourless and only smells when broken down by bacteria. Most sweat glands are found under the armpits, in the genital area and on the feet. Sweat production can be affected by physical exertions and anxiety or stress. Some young people find it difficult to get used to sweating more. The activity "Personal care: – daily washing" (pages 110–111) reinforces the areas that need daily washing. It is good practice to change the clothes in direct contact with these areas regularly too, so clean underwear and socks every day.

You can also use the "Puberty pack" (pages 172–174) and "Personal hygiene: Products tricks and tips" (pages 158–159) to introduce different strategies and products.

Males also need to understand that the foreskin of the penis needs to be gently retracted from time to time, to clean underneath – in the bath is ideal. Females need to understand that the vagina is self-cleaning and only the external organs need washing.

3.19–3.23 HAIRCARE

Encourage your child to help brush your hair and to brush dolls' hair as a preliminary to brushing their own hair. Children's brushes are often preferred as they are very soft, but these brushes do not untangle knots and do not stimulate the scalp.

The best children's hairbrushes will take into consideration the sensitivity of a child's scalp, the size of their hands and make it easier for her to regularly tackle any knots.

The most generally reliable children's brush is the TangleTeezer™ which gets through knots without causing undue distress, suits all hair types and can be used on wet or dry hair. The design is ergonomic, specific to children's hand size and shape.

Good brushing and combing can reduce head lice infestations, reducing lice circulation, preventing multiplication, and reducing the opportunity for the creation of safer nesting areas. Head lice are prevalent amongst younger children in primary schools. The hardest area to brush is in the nape of the neck, which mats quite easily and can allow colonies of lice to develop. Show your child how to tip her head forward and brush from the nape forward. Doing this with conditioner in the hair over the wash basin, makes it more difficult for lice to grip and removes them from hair. Should you become aware of lice, ask your pharmacist to recommend products as they rotate them round to reduce developing immunity.

Putting hair bobbles in can be quite tricky, so try with dolls first or a Girl's World™ styling head if you have one, or allow your child to put the bobbles in your hair, before trying on their own. The stretch and twist manoeuvre requires considerable dexterity. If your child can't master bobbles, consider stretchy bands or wide slides or barrettes instead. After PE the hair can often need readjusting.

After the onset of puberty hair may become greasy, quickly increasing the need for washing. However, too much washing can simply stimulate the scalp to produce more oil, so use a small amount of gentle shampoo and consider alternating with dry shampoo. See the "Supporting your child with hair washing" handout on pages 154–155 for ideas on helping you child take responsibility for their own hair washing or give them the "How to wash your hair" activity sheet (pages 108–109) to guide them through the process.

3.24 INDEPENDENT BATHING OR SHOWERING

The point you allow your child to bathe or shower independently is entirely down to the ability of your child to stay safe, and your personal preference. That said, as your child matures and they start going through some of the physical changes outlined above, they may wish for more privacy. Consider if your child can climb safely in and out of the bathtub.

Have you got a bathmat in the bath and a non-slip mat on the floor where they get out?

If they are physically big enough and have well-developed motor skills, can you let them bathe alone? If you have all these things in place, there is no reason your child cannot bathe independently, although of course, you will need to have gone through the processes and be sure they can wash themselves properly beforehand.

If your child fills the bath themselves, teach them to run cold water first and keep checking the temperature. You may also need to control the amount of bubble bath that is used, but this can be regulated with a dispenser or by using bath bombs.

If you are anxious, try allowing them to get in and out without water in the bath first. You could also add an additional rail to the side of the bath for extra security. There are some inexpensive suction ones that will secure to the bath or to tiles, or you could seek advice from an **Occupational Therapist**.

3.25 TEETH

By now your child will be starting to lose their deciduous (baby) teeth and the adult teeth will be coming in, some may well have already arrived. Now, more than ever, it becomes important that they look after their teeth.

Hygiene issues seem to be more common in children with sensory integration or autism issues and it can be frustrating to discover a child with **pica** will put almost anything in his mouth, other than a toothbrush!

It can be hard to get to the root of the problem. Is it the taste, is it the texture, or just the whole idea? All you can do is offer alternatives to see if one actually works.

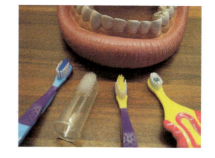

Poor teeth reflect badly on the individual, but can also be a terrible source of pain, particularly if your child also resists attending or receiving treatment from the dentist. The "Personal hygiene: Products, tips, and tricks" handout in the appendices on pages 158–159 offers a range of different suggestions and products you can try with your child. There are many different toothbrushes and pastes you can try.

If you are leaving your child to brush their own teeth, make sure they can identify the toothpaste. It should be recognisable by smell – but just in case, consider putting an elastic band around it to distinguish it from other tubes. If you use the same brand regularly, you can put a bit of sticky braille on the lid and swap the lids over when you open a new pack.

3.26 SPOTS, CLEANSING, TONING, AND MAKEUP

Young children don't need makeup, but often they like to mimic older siblings and friends. If you feel you child is old enough and are willing to permit makeup, there are some very good videos on YouTube. For the time being however, you may prefer to permit just a little eye shadow or a lip gloss, both of which can be gently applied with the finger.

You may want to consider whether this is also the point to introduce proper makeup remover – the pads work really well with limited vision, and also cleansing and toning. There is a knack to placing a cotton pad over the top of an open bottle and tipping it to get the fluid onto it, without the contents going everywhere. Practise with an old – not full – bottle with a tray underneath to reduce the mess if it does go wrong.

Spots can start at any point once puberty has begun and is not necessarily any reflection on your child's cleanliness. That said, dirty skin may increase the risk of spots becoming infected, so encourage a good cleaning regime and seek advice if the problem persists. Although your child will be self-conscious about spots, most young people get them at some point and covering with makeup is only going to make them worse in the long run.

4: Social skills

4.00	**Social skills**
4.01	Play card, table, and board games
4.02	Turn taking
4.03	Self-esteem
4.04	Resilience
4.05	Social interaction rules
4.06	Use appropriate language to others
4.07	Follow instructions
4.08	Early negotiation skills
4.09	Appropriate interruption
4.10	Body language
4.11	Gesture
4.12	Audible voice
4.13	Eye contact
4.14	Friendships

DOI: 10.4324/9781003280132-7

Activities to work on these skills

Personal space

Conversation starter: All about me

Conversation starter: 25 things to say

Hello, goodbye, and interruptions

Handouts

Conversation starter: Let's play board and table games

Four simple rules for good social interaction

Online: How to talk to someone you like

Useful websites and books

Talkabout for Children, Developing Social Skills Alex Kelly (ages 4–11)

Talkabout for Teenagers/Developing Social and Emotional Communication Skills Alex Kelly and Brian Sains (ages 11–19)

Socially Speaking: Pragmatic Social Skills Programme for Pupils with Mild to Moderate Learning Disabilities Paperback LDA 1998 by Alison Schroeder (Author), Jacqueline M. Jomain (Illustrator)

You're a Star A Guide to Self- Esteem Poppy O'Neill Vie (8 March 2018)

Bully-Proof Kids Stella O'Malley Swiftpress 2022

www.understood.org/en/friends-feelings/common-challenges/picking-up-on-social-cues/video
-how-to-teach-your-child-about-personal-space
www.nhs.uk/mental-health/self-help/tips-and-support/raise-low-self-esteem/
www.kidscape.org.uk/advice/advice-for-young-people/dealing-with-bullying/
www.nspcc.org.uk/what-is-child-abuse/types-of-abuse/bullying-and-cyberbullying/
www.childline.org.uk/info-advice/bullying-abuse-safety/types-bullying/
www.ceop.police.uk/Safety-Centre/

4.01–4.02 DEVELOPING SOCIAL SKILLS THROUGH GAMES

Just because your child is a little older, it doesn't mean you should stop playing with them. Playing card and table or board games are great family activities that engender natural conversation and provide you with opportunities to model conversation, demonstrate appropriate behaviour and introduce negotiation skills without your child being aware. It also provides wonderful opportunities to develop social skills in preparation for using them outside the home.

Games help your child ask and answer questions, give and follow instructions, take turns, use manners, learn patience and the importance of being fair, all of which are essential for good social interaction. Games that enable your child to develop skills can boost self-esteem, and losing develops resilience.

There are many games that are suitable for children and young people and enable you to address social skills. Games that require turn taking are particularly good, as are those that require some negotiation.

Specially adapted games	**Accessible without or with minor adaptation**
Connect 4*	Buckaroo
Dominoes *	Crocodile Dentist
Playing cards *	Jenga
Scrabble *	Kerplunk
Uno *	Pop-up Pirate
	Beetle Game
	Chess
Accessible with own adaptations	**Learning games**
Whatever Next	Socially Speaking
Monopoly	Social skills 6 board games
Sound bingo	Chill Chat Challenge

Those with * are currently available in accessible tactile versions.

You can make many games accessible by adding tactile dice, by making the most of any vision the child has by giving him the counter easiest for him to see, placing the board close and within his field of vision and by designating the adult as the card or challenge reader. Many "race to the finish" board games can be improved by adding **Tacti-Mark**™. A blob of Blu Tack™ on the counters makes them more difficult to accidentally dislodge. It may be worth asking your **Habilitation Specialist** or Sensory Team if they have any games you can borrow. Services may have a variety of tactile adapted games that were previously available, but have been discontinued, including Snakes and Ladders, Ludo, Tic-Tac-Toe (Noughts and Crosses), Battleships, Connect 4, Chess and Draughts. Many of the Orchard Toys™ learning games can be individually adapted with **Tacti-Mark**™ and sticky Braille, so check with the teams before undertaking adaptations yourself.

Whilst adaptations can make a game more accessible to youngsters with SVI, it should not weight competition in their favour. Children need to experience disappointment in order to learn from it and grow. If they don't experience losing or loss generally, they won't be able to empathise with others when they lose. It teaches the child how to be a good sport and to accept loss gracefully. This is best experienced first in the home, where any overreaction can be modulated, rather than amongst a room full of classmates. It can help children learn coping skills, encourage them to consider playing strategically, and acknowledge and learn from mistakes. The result is that your child becomes more confident and resilient.

4.03 SELF-ESTEEM

The NHS website provides a simple definition of self-esteem.

> *Self-esteem is the opinion we have of ourselves.*
> *When we have healthy self-esteem, we tend to feel positive about ourselves and about life in general. It makes us better able to deal with life's ups and downs.*
> *When our self-esteem is low, we tend to see ourselves and our life in a more negative and critical light. We also feel less able to take on the challenges that life throws at us.*
>
> *NHS website*

Many things affect self-esteem. Unless it is addressed early, CYPVI often have poor body awareness and poor self-image. It can be difficult to develop a strong self-image when you can't see.

Self-esteem can be affected by experiences. Positive enjoyable experiences can boost self-esteem, as can positive reinforcement and praise. But trauma or upsetting experiences, like being bullied, can impact negatively on self-esteem. The changes that occur during puberty can also adversely affect self-esteem. To help your child combat unhealthy ideas about body image, consider the language you use about yourself. Every time you talk about dieting or criticise your own body, you send a negative message to your child. Stress being healthy and strong rather than raising weight issues.

Much changes during the timeframe covered in this book and children can find it difficult coping with both the changes and challenges they encounter. Children begin to form their own close friendships, as opposed to playing with cousins or the children of parents' friends. They may then begin to be influenced less by parents and carers and become subject to peer pressure for the first time. On top of this, the physical and emotional changes in the early stages of puberty, together with an emergent awareness of attraction to others, adds to the sense of confusion. In some children, this can affect self-esteem.

Children with low self-esteem or confidence, may hide themselves away from social situations, stop trying new things, and avoid things they find challenging. It can be difficult to establish low esteem with any certainty, as it can manifest in different ways in different circumstances. Most children will have periods of anxiety or low self-esteem from time to time. There are a number of publications and websites with tips and activities to help boost your child's self-esteem and confidence but seek help from your GP in the first instance if you have serious concerns.

4.04 RESILIENCE

Resilience is the term for the ability to adapt and bounce back when things don't go as planned. According to the *Cambridge Dictionary* it is "the ability to be happy, successful, etc. again after something difficult or bad has happened".

A positive, growth mindset develops resilience. Teach a *can do* mentality. Everyone can make mistakes, but we can all learn from them and grow. Failure helps you learn what doesn't work and develops problem solving skills. Encourage your child to think through and resolve their own problems, perhaps with support initially, but ensure it is support and not overprotection. Help your child identify her own emotions and recognise the emotions of others, so she can apply appropriate responses.

Bullying is common among tweens. It is part of pushing boundaries and finding your place in the scheme of things. Teach your child how to handle bullying – a resilient child will cope with bullying better. Tell her to speak up and tell the bully to stop in a calm voice, walk away, and stay away, and talk to a trusted adult. It's not telling tales but acting responsibly to speak out if you are being bullied. Peer pressure emerges as your child approaches the teenage years. It is more subtle and involves doing something that one wouldn't normally do to fit in with friends. However, peer pressure can be both positive and negative. Often children just want to fit in and be cool, and some challenges can allow personal growth. Unfortunately, some children are more likely to be negatively influenced by peers. These include children who have poor self-esteem, feel they have few friends, or have special needs.

Unfortunately, children and young people who look or act differently are often the target of bullies. Never accept bullying or think that it will just settle down. Schools should have robust policies in place to deal with bullying, but try and equip your child to deal with low level bullying themselves. This is generally more effective and prevents it escalating. Bullying can take many different forms, so it is not always easy to identify or address. If you are concerned for your child, speak to their school, and look at the advice on the webpages at the start of this section. Kidscape offers advice to children and a parent advice line, and the NSPCC provides advice and support to parents and dedicated child support on Childline. *Bully-Proof Kids* by Stella O'Malley is also full of practical tools to help you help your child grow up confident and resilient.

4.05–4.09 THE RULES OF SOCIAL INTERACTION

Social interaction should change depending on where the child is and to whom they are talking. They need to know the difference between formal and informal situations and modify behaviour accordingly. Good social skills are based on unwritten rules that are often missed out in teaching social skills, simply because they are unwritten and mostly delivered as an afterthought. Whilst the choice of appropriate phrases may vary, the rules apply in all situations from the formal interview down to playground interactions. Introduce the idea of shaking hands and using other greeting gestures, highlighting when they are most appropriate. She will need to be able to follow and apply a series of instructions for this to work.

Four simple rules for good social interaction

#1 Meet and greet politely

In the VI world, we tend to spend a great deal of time encouraging other people to "see" the young person with VI and address them directly. We put the onus on others to initiate conversations and start introductions, but **CYPVI** need to be able to do this too.

Greet people appropriately. Say "Hello," "Hi," "Good morning," "How do you do,"[1] "Pleased to meet you," as appropriate.

Simple exchange. A basic conversation should follow introductions. This could be a reflection on the weather, the location, or an exchange of compliments.

A clear ending. You may need to contrive an excuse to depart, so say something like "I've got to go now." Alternatively, the conversation may have come to an end, so use "Goodbye," "'bye," or refer back to your opening greeting. Don't leave the other person hanging. If they too have a vision impairment, they may not even realise you have gone.

#2 Take turns

Listen to what the other person is saying. Establish eye contact if you can.

Don't interrupt. Wait for an appropriate gap in the conversation. A conversation is an exchange, and you need to take turns to speak. Some turns may be longer than others. If only one person speaks it is not a conversation.

If you need to interrupt – pick your time carefully.

Respond appropriately. This may mean nodding and smiling rather than saying very much.

#3 Pay attention

Show that you are listening.

Use your own body language to convey interest in what is being said. Nod occasionally, Smile at good or happy things and frown at the bad.

Establish eye contact if you can.

Listen to the intonation, which tells you more about how the other person feels.

#4 Think

Think about what you do and what you say.

Don't be unnecessarily rude. Apologise if necessary. Follow instructions and directions. Ask for help if necessary.

---

1 "How do you do" is defined as a polite greeting used when first introduced to someone in a formal setting. The formal response is to repeat the phrase back. Whilst regarded as outdated, it is still used in business and formal settings and needs to be understood if not actively used.

> **Don't touch people or things without permission**. Apologise if you collide, even if you think it was the other person's fault.
>
> **Recognise personal space**. Personal space can be difficult for CYPVI who may need to be closer to see the person they are talking to, or because of little or no vision may not realise how close they are. See the "Personal space" activity sheet (pages 122–123).

Additionally, your child will have to learn about appropriate interruption. Whilst it is polite to wait for the speaker to stop talking, sometimes it becomes necessary to interrupt. See the "Hello, goodbye, and interruptions" activity sheet on pages 119–121 for more on this theme.

For a conversation to develop further and flow rather than be stilted, emotional intelligence is required. This is defined as a person's ability to express and manage feelings appropriately while respecting the feelings of others. It's a set of skills that children can begin learning at any age.

There are five main aspects of emotional intelligence which, when developed, lead to children becoming emotionally literate. In his book *Emotional Intelligence, why it can matter more than IQ,* Daniel Goleman identifies:

✓ Knowing emotions – a child recognises a feeling as it happens

✓ Managing emotions – a child has ways of reassuring themselves when they feel anxious or upset

✓ Self-motivation – a child is in charge of their emotions, rather than controlled by them

✓ Empathy – a child is aware of what another person is feeling

✓ Handling relationships – a child is able to build relationships with others

There are some circumstances peculiar to those with vision impairment that require specific skills.

Negotiation skills are vital if your child is going out and about independently. At some point it is likely that she will need to either accept or refuse help politely. There is a knack to this, and the exchange is best rehearsed or even scripted to address different scenarios. Jokes abound about people being crossed over roads they don't want to cross.

Why did the red-nosed reindeer help the old lady cross the road?

It would have been Rudolph him not to!

But it's not funny at all if your child is taken off her known route. Even if accepting help, it is vital the child stays in control of the situation. If she declines the help, it is important she refuses it in such a way that the person is not put off ever offering again. The other person may have hesitated for some time before approaching and offering assistance.

Sometimes the help that is required is not offered. This may then require the child speaking into the void in the hope of securing assistance. This is incredibly hard for young people to learn. It is best rehearsed at tills or customer service desks in shops, where there is a reasonable expectation that someone is there and will respond, but it is still daunting. It is important to develop a clear audible speaking voice through modelling and role play, before engaging directly with the general public. It is too easy for the student to drop her head and mumble.

4.10–4.13 GOOD VERBAL AND NON-VERBAL COMMUNICATION

Dropping the head and mumbling conveys a poor impression from the outset. The head tilt mutes the voice further. Encourage your child to find her BIG voice – not shouting – the one she might use to yell at siblings, but one that can be heard from the other side of the counter in a shop. Rehearse it at home and then prompt if required in a variety of settings.

Encourage the child to maintain good head posture and turn her face towards any voice. This will at least give the impression of establishing eye contact. This can be refined by gazing just above where the voice is coming from, but it takes practice. Now smile! Rightly or wrongly, this makes the other person feel more comfortable and makes it more likely she will secure the assistance she needs.

The 7–38–55 rule

The 7–38–55 rule is all about the communication of emotions. Coined by Professor Albert Mehrabian in his book *Silent Messages* (1971) the concept is now frequently applied in negotiation training. He postulated that 7% of meaning is communicated through spoken word, 38% through tone of voice, and 55% through body language. For the majority of the population, tone of voice and body language are actually more important than the words that are actually being said. And whilst this research relates specifically to the communication of emotions and feelings, it demonstrates clearly why **CYPVI** may struggle in social settings. Those with very low or no vision, are more likely to need to be taught to pick up and utilise the nuances of conversation.

Using the right intonation can actually change the meaning of your words. As you speak, your voice gets louder and softer, placing emphasis on certain parts. The tones or notes of your voice are called its pitch, and the change in pitch is what we call intonation.

There are two main English intonation patterns:

✓ **Falling:** when your voice lowers its pitch at the end of the sentence. This is usually used for statements and questions that require complex answers, not a simple yes or no. Falling intonation implies speech coming to an end

✓ **Rising:** when your voice raises its pitch at the end of the sentence. This is usually used when you're asking a yes or no question or to show disbelief or anger. Rising intonation invites the other party to speak

But speech patterns vary in different locations. According to Dr Rod Walters in the BBC article of 8 June 2006, the Welsh have musical accents, with distinct intonation. *"While there are other British Isles accents that have their own recognisable intonations, for example the Glasgow, Belfast, Birmingham and Liverpool accents, none of these are phonetically the same as Welsh accents."* http://news.bbc.co.uk/1/hi/wales/5056236.stm

When the way the words are intoned and enunciated conveys meaning, rather than the actual words that are used, the additional input from body language and gesture reinforces understanding. Much of what people say is reinforced by gesture and body language, without access to this the child is dependent on intonation and pitch to convey the meaning of the words being spoken. Spend time reading out loud together to practice delivering content with expression and intonation.

Take your child to extra-curricular and leisure activities to broaden her horizons. An active life will give her something to talk about and enable her to meet more people to model behaviour on and develop her own social skills. Encourage her to use gestures to reinforce what she is saying and if she has some useful vision, look for such gestures in others.

4.14 FRIENDSHIPS

Younger children benefit from orchestrated playdates, from socialising with cousins or with the children of their parents' friends. In these sheltered groups they start to learn social skills and norms, modelling behaviour on the adults or more socially adept children in the group. Sometimes other parents are wary about taking care of a child with vision impairment, so offer to stay or invite that child to come and play at your house first.

Once in school, children start to develop their own friendship groups. If your child struggles to build friendships, speak to the school or one of the specialists supporting your child to see what interventions can be put in place initially to start the process off. Creating buddy systems in school, where the buddy advocates on behalf of the child or draws her into their own friendship group can prove successful. Sometimes the other children can be afraid of engaging with the child with VI, worrying about doing or saying the wrong thing. The **Habilitation Specialist** or **QTVI** can organise peer awareness training to reduce the anxiety of classmates and encourage normal social interaction and if circumstances warrant, other parents could be invited too, so that their fears can be allayed.

Children with sight impairment also benefit from the opportunity to meet up and socialise with other CYPVI. Here they can talk about shared experiences and strategies to deal with the issues that impact on them. Your **Vision Support Team** will probably organise activities, but there are a number of other local and national organisations that offer activities. Most organisations have websites as well as a strong presence on social media, but many are listed in the online "Accessing activities and support" handout.

As they mature, friendships become increasingly important, and the views of parents and carers can be side-lined in favour of peer pressure. Having friends and feeling connected to a group gives older children a sense of belonging and being valued, which helps develop self-esteem and confidence. Friendships also help children learn important social and emotional skills, like being sensitive to other people's thoughts, feelings, and wellbeing. Tweens and children in middle childhood tend to stay in single-sex friendship groups, although there are always exceptions.

If you have concerns about your child's social skills, there are a number of activities in this book. However, you may also find it helpful to investigate the *Talkabout* series or the *Socially Speaking* book mentioned at the start of this section. Both of these can be easily adapted to be accessible to CYPVI.

Concerns about your child's understanding of social situations or use of language should be raised in school or with a **speech and language therapist**.

5: Time and organisational skills

5.00	**Time and organisational skills**
5.01	Days, months and seasons
5.02	Elapsing time, secs, mins and hours
5.03	Time – digital
5.04	Time – analogue
5.05	Talking time devices
5.06	Reading a school timetable
5.07	Organisational skills
5.08	Identify own items, coat, shoes, bag, etc.
5.09	Pack a school bag
5.10	Clothes storage

DOI: 10.4324/9781003280132-8

Activities to work on these skills

Simple timer games

Meet Alexa

Prerequisite Skills

A basic understanding of time

Handouts

Using Alexa

Tactile marking and labelling

Useful websites and books

www.partsight.org.uk/shop/diaries-calendars

https://shop.rnib.org.uk/house/stationery/calendars-and-diaries

Time is a particularly difficult concept for children who have no ability to distinguish between day and night, and many children with vision impairments only develop this skill late. When there is nothing going on and you can't see, time passes very slowly.

5.01 DAYS, MONTHS, AND SEASONS

If he struggles with any of these areas, refer back to *Supporting Life Skills for Young Children*. It is important that he can anticipate and understand seasonal adjustments in the weather, and what clothing he might need to wear. When you go out and the weather is significant, for instance with crunchy leaves underfoot or snow, it is easier to draw your child's attention to the seasons. Check also that he knows own date of birth (not just as birthday) and can give it to a third party.

Does he really understand the difference between night and day? This is a very difficult concept to grasp if you have no vision, particularly for younger children. Don't allow your child to blur the boundaries between night and day. Provide structure and routine so that the child knows approximately what time things happen. Waking up is followed by getting dressed and eating breakfast. The school day is punctuated by breaks and lunchtime, and evening play should calm into a soothing bedtime routine. Ensure your child knows playing is not acceptable at night. If your child still struggles with sleep at night, speak to your GP, paediatrician, or one of the organisations listed under "**Sleep**" in the Glossary (page 236).

5.02–5.05 TIME

We are moving increasingly into a world where digital timings are used, but from a habilitation perspective an understanding of an analogue clock is very useful. Here in the UK, we use the clock face to give navigational directions and to assist people finding the food on the plate. At the very least your child needs to know about the clock face, the layout of the numbers, and how they are used in relation to him. If he can actually tell the time using an analogue clock, so much the better.

The clock face is laid out on the "Locating food on a plate" handout (pages 182–183), or you can invest in one of the many teaching clocks on the market with a talking feature. You can add Braille numbers onto the clock using a Braille dymo to make it fully accessible.

Most talking time devices use digital timing and so don't teach about analogue time, so you will need a teaching clock to do this. You child may need timings like "a quarter to three", or "ten to five", explaining in some detail as they don't correlate easily with digital time. If they have started reading the time from digital devices, they may find analogue complicated. There are some lovely clear "telling the time" activity cards commercially available to practise the calculations between analogue and digital or you can make your own, with a set of digital times and an analogue clock face with accessible hands to set the times on.

Elapsing time can also be a problem for some CYPVI. Consider playing games that require a timer to try and demonstrate how time passes. This can be through the "Simple timer games" on pages 124–125, or by adding a timer challenge into other games.

Build timings into everyday life, by using egg timers or an audible timer for tooth brushing. Bake fairy cakes together, that cook in a relatively short time, and get your child to set the timer. Encourage the use of devices that offer updates on the time remaining, like Alexa or other home devices, or mobile phones. Alexa offers a wide range of alarms, reminders and countdown timers that you can use to reinforce time and organisational skills, some of which are included in the "Using Alexa" activity sheet on page 126.

Whilst its great fun to use Alexa as a reminder and calendar, also give your child a physical calendar of his own, if he can access it. If he can't see commercial ones, The Partially Sighted Society and the RNIB produce large print calendars and diaries and the RNIB also produces Braille versions. Sometimes, writing things down and crossing off the days builds a better understanding of time.

Encourage your child to wear a watch that he can use independently. In school pupils are often not allowed to use mobile phones, so wearing a watch allows him to check on elapsed time and anticipate events coming up. There are lots of big clear clock faces, large print digital and tactile watches, as well as some that vibrate to give the time silently. Talking watches can be quite disruptive in school, so make sure it is not set to make regular time announcements.

5.06 TIMETABLES

Learning to use a school timetable can be a complex skill, but it is useful when your child moves to secondary school, as not only does he have to know what his next lesson is, he has to know where it is. The school should offer his timetable in whatever format he can access. He will need a copy at home and a more durable copy to carry round. If he can read print, a laminated timetable is best.

Many students (particularly those who find organisational skills challenging) opt to carry everything every day. This can make backpacks *very* heavy. If your child is a Braillist it could mean many large books and folders. This can cause multiple issues. Firstly, carrying such a heavy bag is not good for the back and can create problems for life. The Braille dots can crush when pressed together for long periods and it can be difficult to find anything in the bag. And the bag can disturb the child's centre of balance, putting them at greater risk if jolted or when climbing or descending stairs.

Even lower down the school simple timetables can help your child prepare for the day. You can create your own based on known activities, like Monday is swimming, Tuesday is library, and Friday is PE. You can put this together in large print, using widget or Makaton symbols or with objects of reference. If you are using objects of reference, speak to the school to ensure you are using the same tactile references to avoid confusion. Always look forward with objects of reference and watch out for things that may become redundant if your child progresses. For instance, if you use arm bands to represent swimming, your child may be confused if he no longer needs them to swim. Instead keep his old swimming trunks as the object of reference – the material is quite identifiable, and trunks are a constant. Use pumps for PE as the actual activity may change.

5.07–5.10 ORGANISATIONAL SKILLS

To understand organisation, your child needs to understand sequences. He needs to know what the ultimate objective of any task is, and all the smaller sequences in between to achieve that objective. In order to succeed he may need tasks breaking down into component parts and he may need support, through modelling, scaffolding or verbal directions. Begin organisational skills activities as joint ventures. Ask your child to help put their own toys or gadgets away and gradually make it their responsibility. If the task is too big it can become overwhelming, so make sure it is achievable. Make sure everything has a designated "home" that your child knows about.

Moving on from toys, ask him to help you bring the shopping in and put it away. This helps him learn that everyone has responsibilities to put things away, and also gives him a better idea of where to look for things once he progresses to making his own drinks or snacks. It will also help him to identify different foodstuffs and learn where they should be stored. You may need to be precise about some foodstuffs as the same thing can be stored differently, depending on how it is preserved. Take peas, for instance, they can be fresh and stored in a refrigerator, frozen and stored in the freezer, or tinned and stored in the cupboard.

The less vision a child has, the more important it is that he is systematic from an early age. Everything needs its own place and needs to be returned there after use. Floor space and surfaces should remain as uncluttered as possible to avoid confusion and potential damage. Your home may not be large enough for him to have his own room, but he should at least have designated areas and feel secure in that knowledge that his siblings will not move his possessions, making it difficult for him to find them.

Where possible, clothes should be labelled so your child can identify his own clothes at home or school, but particularly if he wears a uniform for school as personal items become harder to identify. There is more on this in the section on Advanced dressing (pages 22–28).

If your child needs his clothes putting out, then be systematic about where you put them, as consistency is key. If possible, establish places for your child to keep and access his clothes independently. Label drawers so the contents are identifiable and get him to help put things away so he develops a memory of where they go.

Work out your own systems at home, so your child knows where to find his uniform, or appropriate clothing for the day. That could be on a chair or on top of a chest of drawers. Once he has mastered the dressing skills, then you can consider progressing to selecting appropriate clothes for himself. Teach him to return clothes to the chair the right way round, so he could put them on again. Check he can hang clothes securely on a peg. Some schools use lockers too, so teach him how to fold clothing so it is wearable afterwards. See the section on Household chores (pages 80–85) for more information on folding.

6–7: Money and shopping skills

6.00	**Money skills**
6.01	Coin recognition
6.02	Note identification
6.03	Place in value order
6.04	Simple value calculations
6.05	Simple change calculation
6.06	Using a calculator
6.07	Bank card use
6.08	Apple Pay
6.09	Intro to ATM
7.00	**Shopping skills**
7.01	Shopping/cafe simulation activities
7.02	Shop identification – visual
7.03	Shop identification – alternate cues
7.04	Awareness of what shops might sell
7.05	Awareness of customer services
7.06	Dealing with store staff appropriately/asking for help
7.07	Eye contact
7.08	Using shopping list – print, Braille, electronic, pictographic
7.09	Locating price tickets
7.10	Reading and understanding price ticket
7.11	Selecting goods
7.12	Location of counter/tills in store
7.13	Paying for goods supported
7.14	Paying no assistance
7.15	Self-service tills
7.16	Pack shopping bag
7.17	Carrying purchases
7.18	Remember items bought
7.19	Remember price for third party

DOI: 10.4324/9781003280132-9

Activities to work on these skills

Money skills -Cut and paste coins in value order

How many Pounds?

Find the prices

Prerequisite skills

Good tactile discrimination

Handouts

Useful websites and books

www.link.co.uk/consumers/locator/ where to find talking ATMs

www.finder.com/uk/better-debit-cards-for-kids debit cards from age 11

www.finder.com/uk/credit-card-options-teens prepaid cards from age 6

www.moneysavingexpert.com/banking/cards-for-under-18s/

6.01–6.06 MONEY HANDLING

If your child is still of an age where he enjoys playing shops, ensure he gets to handle real money as much as possible, rather than using toy replacements. The feel and weight are completely different. Remember copper coins have smooth edges and silver coins have ridged edges. The 20p and 50p have seven sides but are different sizes and weights. Practise sorting coins into copper and silver, then sorting into each different denomination. Then work on the relative value of each coin and practise finding a particular coin from a pot and then from a purse or wallet. Finding the right money from your purse in a pressured situation at the till can be difficult. The more practice the child has, the better he will be at it. Give him a wallet or purse that opens up well to make all the coins accessible. If he carries notes, keep them separate according to value.

Allow your child to hand money over in shops, so he gets used to handling money in real situations and learns the till procedures. Small local shops are best to start with, when you haven't got a weekly shop loaded on the conveyer belt and a long queue behind you. Give your child small amounts of pocket money if you can and allow him to spend it. This will start to help him learn the cost of goods and calculate what he can afford. You can, if you wish, tie the amount of pocket money into household chores that he completes.

Aim to buy one thing initially and then gradually increase the complexity of adding prices together and calculating change. If your child can recognise money but can't do complex calculations he can use the calculator on his phone to avoid being embarrassed by a short-fall at the till.

Each of the polymer notes produced by the Bank of England are different colours and different sizes. The higher the value, the bigger the note. The larger notes have groupings of four dots, to help indicate the value. This is not Braille, you just count the groupings.

£5 colour turquoise/blue. On the front of the note, you can feel raised print on the words "Bank of England" and in the bottom right corner, around the number 5. It does not have any raised dots.

£10 colour orange. On the front of the note, you can feel raised print on the words "Bank of England" and in the bottom right corner, around the number 10. There are two clusters of raised dots in the top left corner (2 groups of 4 dots)

£20 colour purple. On the front of the note, you can feel raised print on the words "Bank of England" and in the bottom right corner, over the smaller window. On the front of the note (the side with raised print), there are three clusters of raised dots in the top left corner (3 groups of 4 dots).

£50 colour red. On the front of the note, you can feel raised print on the words "Bank of England" and there are four clusters of raised dots in the top left corner. £50 notes are not in common usage and many people are wary of accepting them because of the high value.

Bank of Scotland notes are similar colours and sizes, but the picture designs vary. The same dot sequence is used on polymer notes.

Bank of Ireland colours and pictures vary from those produced by the Bank of England, but they also use the same dot sequence.

If the child's hands are large enough, you can match note size to particular fingers. You can also use apps or the Cobolt NoteReader to identify notes and then fold them differently for identification in the wallet.

6.07–6.09 ELECTRONIC BANKING

Although the use of cash reduced during the Covid restrictions, usage is rising again. However, as a result of the wider acceptance of cards, the restrictions that were formerly in place, discouraging the use of cards for small amounts has largely disappeared. This means your child can pay for small items of shopping, pay their bus fare, or undertake numerous activities without ever resorting to cash. This brings many advantages to **CYPVI**, who are no longer required to search through coins in a hurry or locate and put the exact change into the bus fare collector. However, it can also leave them vulnerable to unscrupulous people who have more scope to overcharge or who may try and steal card information.

It is a really good idea to open a bank account for your child, even if just to hold birthday money temporarily. It introduces the idea of saving and helps your child become aware of banking processes. Banking apps change all the time, so consult groups like VITalk to find out which is currently the most VI accessible, if your child is going to have control over their own money. However, banks do not offer spending services to CYP under 11, so you may also like to consider other options.

Prepaid credit cards are available to youngsters as young as 6. Many of these cards come with contactless payments and allow in-store or online purchases. You preload an amount on the card and can only spend that balance. It works really well for pocket money spending and to help build an understanding of money.

Some prepaid cards have an annual or monthly fee, but they may provide more services, like child and parent apps, the ability to draw cash from ATMs and may be accepted in more locations.

GoHenry and Rooster are examples of chargeable cards. The GoHenry app allows you to set up regular payments, reward chores, and restrict where and how much money can be spent. It is quite widely accepted and allows cash to be withdrawn from ATMs.

HyperJar is an example of a free prepaid card. It lets you put money in different jars for different purposes and you can get different spending permissions on each jar. Once your child is over 13, you can add their HyperJar card to Apple Pay and Google Pay (this is currently the only pocket money card you can do this with). However, parents have to have their own HyperJar account too, and cash cannot be withdrawn from ATMs.

Consider all the options before you choose, using the up-to-date information on the Money Saving Expert website – www.moneysavingexpert.com/banking/cards-for-under-18s/

Apple Pay

To reduce the need to carry a card, you may also like to consider Apple Pay (or Google Pay on an Android phone). Follow the instructions in settings to set up Apple Pay. If your iPhone has Face ID, double-click the side button. Authenticate with Face ID or enter your passcode. (Face ID can be difficult to use with little or no vision and requires considerable practice getting distance and angles right.) If your iPhone has Touch ID, rest your finger on the Touch ID sensor. Hold the top of your iPhone near the contactless reader until you see "Done" and a tick on the display or hear the confirmation beep. Apple Pay is fully accessible with VoiceOver.

ATMs

Many banks now provide talking ATMs for customers. This allows greater independence and reduces the need to go into your local branch to draw cash. Your child will need to carry his own earphones in order to be able to access the speech. Any earphones will do, and a cheap pair often work better than ones with a built-in microphone that come with a mobile phone.

You can use the ATM at any bank, although you may want to be wary of ATMs not attached to banks that may charge to withdraw cash. See if your bank provides talking ATM machines and try the one inside the bank first. It will be quieter, and the child will feel less vulnerable than outside, plus it means that there will be a member of staff around if he encounters difficulties. If he chooses to use the ATM outside, only put one of the earphones in, so he is still aware of what is going on around him. Remember too, if there is a queue to leave adequate space between himself and the person in front, who may feel uncomfortable drawing cash with someone close, even if they can't see.

Locate the earphone jack – usually to the right of the screen – and follow the spoken instructions. If the sound is not clear, try wiggling the jack until you get clear speech. Like a mobile, there should be a little bump on the 5 on the numerical pad to help locate it. Remember when you set your card up, you can change the pin, so choose a pin that is not only easy to remember, but can be located successfully on the keypad.

If you want to find your nearest talking ATM, go to www.link.co.uk/consumers/locator/ and in the search filters enable Audio Assistance. It defaults onto cash at the till and post offices, so search filters will need changing.

If you are opening a standard bank account for your child, he will need to learn a signature for banking or other official documents. He does not have to write his whole name, just initials will do, but the bank may expect some sort of consistency. Help him become familiar with letter shapes using tactile 3D letters and plastic embossing film (also known as German film). The embossing film rises when drawn on with ballpoint pen or embossing tool, so he can confirm whether the shape he draws resembles the letter. The film must be used on a rubber mat, to ensure the lines raise properly. It can also be used for making simple tactile diagrams. Start with large letters and gradually reduce them down as he becomes more competent, so they fit within a signature guide.

7.00 SHOPPING

7.01–7.04 SHOP IDENTIFICATION AND BASIC SKILLS

If your child is still happy playing shopping games, swap between the roles of shopkeeper and customer, and put real money in his till. Where possible use real packets, so your child becomes familiar with them. Create prices that are accessible to the child both in terms of size and format, but also values that he can comprehend. Everything can be in pennies or even whole pounds at first and gradually move towards more realistic pricing. There are also some Orchard Games around shopping that lend themselves well to adaptation for vision impairment. At school your child may have the opportunity to pay for snacks at break and rehearse the whole shopping scenario.

Whenever you go out, talk about the shops that you pass and the ones you go into. Explain what each store sells and categorise them for him, so he learns what sort of things they might sell. He may be able to identify shops using visual clues, or he may need to use the sounds and smells or tactile clues around him. Many shops can be identified by the smell, some are obvious like coffee shops, bakers, and fishmongers, but shoe shops also have a distinctive

leather smell. You can smell a Lush™ store from some distance away and can use it for navigation purposes. The proximity to pelican crossings, the display baskets, and the distinctive smells outside, all contribute to knowing exactly where you are.

7.05–7.10 IN-STORE SKILLS

There is always a balance between small independent stores and larger supermarkets and department stores. Smaller stores are more personal, tend to be easier to navigate around, and your child will probably feel more comfortable. On the other hand, they tend to be more expensive than the bigger national chain stores and supermarkets and may carry a more limited range. He needs to know about them all, so he can make informed choices. Visit different stores and compare prices using the "Find the prices" activity sheet on page 130.

The shopkeeper in a small store is likely to acknowledge the customer as he walks in and may offer help without being asked. If you have a little local shop you use regularly, make sure you take your child in from time to time, introduce him to staff and build his confidence moving round the store and paying for goods. If the route is feasible, he may eventually be able to go to the store independently to buy snacks, bread or milk. Speak to your **Habilitation Specialist** about the route and when it could be introduced.

In a supermarket the staff are more remote, and whilst they will help, you often have to locate someone and ask for help. Point out staff as you move round the store, indicating what the uniform looks like. This is helpful not only for building shopping skills, but also if your child gets separated from you. Most large supermarkets have a customer service desk, where you can secure assistance with shopping. Some will provide help at any time, others like you to let them know in advance. This would need negotiating with individual stores. Whilst the layout of stores changes, the tills rarely move and provide good information regarding the way out of the store and likely places to find help. Rehearse together how he could ask for help and go to the customer service desk together to discuss how support might work in that particular store. Remind him to look at the staff, and smile, even if he can't see them properly, as this will elicit a more positive response.

Keep your child involved while you are shopping. Give him a small shopping list in a format he can access independently (large print, Braille, on a mini memo, on his phone or use Widgit or pictures). If he can find some products himself, encourage him to do so, otherwise tell him what aisle he is in and talk about the products he will find there. If your child is progressing to independent food shopping, local Coop stores are very helpful. They are big enough to carry a reasonable range, but small enough that the layout can be learned relatively easily. They often operate as part of the local community and get to know customers. If your child likes to use apps, CLEW is very good for navigating indoor environments like supermarkets or shopping malls.

If he can see enough to move round, but can't see prices, ask the supermarket if you can have some old price shelf edge tickets that they are discarding and practise using apps or magnifiers at home to access the information. Once he can do it at home, he will feel more confident in the store. Many people take a photo of the price label and then enlarge it on their phone, but there are many apps that will read out what is on the ticket.

7.11–7.19 PAYING FOR GOODS

Once the shopping has been selected, whether independently or with support, it is time to pay. Tills can usually be located audibly by the constant beeping of the scanners. Your child needs to understand that there might be a queue and how to deal with that. If he uses a long cane, he can gently push it forward at ground level to locate the shoes of the person in front. He should know the prices of the goods he is buying, either from reading the prices, or by using a rough estimate based on his general knowledge of prices. This way he will not be embarrassed at the till by a shortage of funds.

Initially the adult will conduct the transactions and let the child just hand over payment, but over time he should take over more responsibility for loading the shopping onto the conveyer, engaging with the shop assistant and paying for goods. If he is going to undertake completely independent shopping, he will also need to pack his shopping into a bag. For long cane users, backpacks are best, because it keeps the hands free, but he must learn to buy only what he can carry home. He will also need to understand appropriate packing, as failure to put light things to the top and heavy things to the bottom, could result in squashed eggs and bread.

Generally speaking, manned tills are easier for those with severe sight impairments, but if he finds dealing with people difficult and has enough vision to manage, he may prefer self-serve tills. If he is shopping on behalf of others, he will need to either remember what he has bought and how much it cost, so he can report back.

8: Eating and drinking

	EATING AND DRINKING
8.01	Appropriate use of cutlery
8.02	Spoon
8.04	Fork
8.05	Knife
8.06	Adaptive cutlery if required
8.07	System for locating food on plate
8.08	Use of cup
8.09	Use of glass
8.10	Drinking straw
8.11	Table manners

DOI: 10.4324/9781003280132-10

Activities to work on these skills

Prerequisite skills

Bilateral coordination

Hand strength

Handouts

Locating food on a plate

Cutlery skills at mealtimes for children with vision impairment

Useful websites and books

Heathcare Pro is the new online site for NRS, a major supplier of adaptive cutlery, tableware, and other devices:

www.healthcarepro.co.uk/eating-drinking-aids/children-s-eating-drinking

www.howwemontessori.com/how-we-montessori/2019/12/we-road-test-ten-childrens-kitchen -and-chef-knives.html

Now your child is at school there will be an expectation that she can use cutlery appropriately. Lunch times are pressured and short, so staff may not be able to devote a great deal of time to helping your child develop skills. There are few concessions to children in either restaurants or school dining halls, where the expectation will be they will be able to wield full size cutlery.

8.01–8.07 EATING: CUTLERY USE AND LOCATING FOOD

Parents and children can be tempted to avoid the issue by taking packed lunches. If you choose that option, make sure your child can open her lunch box and all packaging. If you pack food into plastic bags, use coloured ones to make them easier for your child to see. Using cutlery is a great life skill and it's worth persevering. If she struggles at school, but not at home, investigate what cutlery is being used in the dining hall.

Refer back to *Supporting Young Children with Vision Impairment and Other Disabilities* for guidance on introducing cutlery and early skills development and for more refined skills use the "Cutlery skills at mealtimes for children with vision impairment" handout on pages 180–181.

Make sure your child is holding the cutlery properly and can locate food on the plate.

Use a combination of "hand over hand" or "hand under hand" together with precise descriptions. Correct placement of the fingers makes it much easier to use cutlery well. Kura Care or Caring Cutlery has dimples that indicate where fingers should sit. They come in a variety of sizes and in contrasting colours. You can put Tacti-Mark™ or flat bumpons onto cutlery to indicate finger placement. Choose cutlery the right size for your child's hands. Quite often you see children holding cutlery too far down the handle, away from the business end. This reduces the control the child has over the cutlery and makes it difficult to exert the required force.

Use the fork to push across the plate to locate food and then stab or spear the food with the fork. Practise this in a non-pressured situation. You can use the clock face to describe where the food is on the plate. This method is described in more detail in the "Locating food on the plate" handout on pages 182–183.

Place the plate so that anything that needs more forceful cutting is close to the child, preferably towards the side that she holds her fork. This gives her confidence searching for the food and allows maximum force to be used when cutting. If you cut too close to the bevelled edge of a plate it may tip. Once located, food should be firmly speared and whilst held in place by the fork, the knife should cut in a sawing motion. You need a considerable amount of pressure to cut some foods. Start with items with lower resistance like banana and progress to potato waffles before attempting meat. Do try and establish which is the child's dominant hand and encourage consistent hand use when using both knife and fork. It takes considerable practice to locate the food, then determine where best to spear it, so you can line the knife up against the fork and cut off a piece small enough to fit in the mouth. You can practise creating different shapes in Playdoh™ while she tries to get the hang of it.

If she has some useful vision, try choosing a plate that contrasts with the food and with the table. Where possible use self-coloured plates and avoid complex patterns that make the plate visually busy. You can place a sheet of Dycem™ underneath the plate to create contrast and stop the plate moving round. You can even use Dycem™ on plates or food trays as it washes well, even in the dishwasher. Reels of Dycem™ can be cut up to go into individual compartments of school meal serving trays to provide maximum contrast. If it's going into a food tray – blue works well – as there is not a lot of blue food!

If your child has very low vision, it is likely to take time for her to become competent in these skills. It may take her longer to eat her food, so make sure the school factors this in and maybe let her go into the dining room first. In primary school there is usually a limited choice of meals and more acceptance of a child needing support with choices, payments, or carrying a tray to a seat. See the "Transition" section (pages 86–93) for more information on dealing with dinner times in secondary schools.

If your child pushes food off the plate or struggles to load the spoon or fork, look into plates with deeper sides that the food can be pushed against to facilitate loading. These do not have to be baby dishes, there are some lovely plates available that will serve the purpose, or you can buy specially designed plates or rims from specialist suppliers like Healthcare Pro.

If your child has a physical difficulty, it is worth obtaining an **Occupational Therapy** assessment, as there are many different types of cutlery and strategies that can help. This could include an assessment for built-up or curved cutlery.

8.08–8.10 DRINKING

Brightly coloured glasses or beakers should stand out and contrast with the surface on which they are placed if your child has useful vision. However, be wary of lightweight plastic beakers that may tip at even a gentle touch. This is even more of an issue if your child uses a liquid level indicator, as the weight makes tipping more likely. Clear glasses can be made more visible with the use of coasters or Dycem™ rings. There is no reason you can't use mugs for cold drinks as well as hot drinks. They are much more stable and come in a wide range of child-friendly designs.

Hot drinks need to be made and served in heat resistant vessels. The handles on mugs just help keep the child's hand that bit further away from the heat source. If you buy hot drinks out and about, although it is a nuisance, it is really worth carrying reusable cups. The cardboard cups takeaway drinks are served in can be very hot and also become malleable if squeezed too tightly.

Most children can manage cups, beakers, and glasses very well, they just need to learn to be controlled with their movements. Encourage your child to reach out at base or tabletop level, rather than lifting the hand to search for the middle or top of the glass. You can place the glass on a tray initially, so that any spillage is contained. Most schools provide water in jugs at lunch time. Teach your child how to pour from a jug (understanding the shape and pouring spout of a jug is key to success). Request that your child has access to a liquid level indicator, if necessary, so she can pour her own drinks.

Children love straws, but pressing down on straws causes the beaker to tip. Inserting small straws into the cartons or pouches so often used in lunch boxes is difficult, and there is a real knack to it. Teach her to recognise the difference between the pointed and the blunt ends.

Locate the insert point – you can feel it. Line the point up, holding the straw in the curled hand, with the thumb over the blunt end. If it's a pouch a gentle squeeze will push the opening up to help you locate it. Jab the straw into the pouch. Because the thumb is over the top of the straw, the contents stay in the pouch instead of spilling. Whatever she's drinking, encourage her to keep her head above the drink. Paper straws bend, squash, and generally deteriorate with sucking and mouthing. You can carry silicone or silicone-tipped metal straws if they work better for your child.

8.11 TABLE MANNERS

All children should be taught good table manners. If these are not addressed from an early age, it can become difficult to address them later when your teen becomes resistant to "nagging". If your child has no useful vision, she cannot model table behaviour on other people and she may not be aware of the potential impact on family and friendships.

✓ Where possible all sit at the table for meals. Mealtimes are a social activity, a time to exchange pleasantries and learn more about conversation and social norms

✓ Hands and, if possible, faces, should be clean coming to the table

✓ Chew with your mouth closed and don't try to talk with your mouth full. This may need explaining, as your child may not realise that you can actually see the food being chewed in the mouth and that it is considered distasteful. Talking with your mouth full also risks spitting food at other people, which is also socially unacceptable

✓ There should be no expectation that she should eat something she really dislikes, but in order to get invited back to a friend's house, it needs to be declined politely. Teach ways to politely decline food at home first, so she is prepared when out and about

✓ Use cutlery appropriately. Don't let your child spear whole food, like sausages or potatoes, and bite it off the fork. If your child struggles with cutting up food, look at the utensils they have. Maybe smaller sized cutlery or even a serrated knife, like the Kuhn Rikon Dog Knife might make it easier.

9–10: Food preparation and simple snacks and drinks

9.00	Food preparation, snacks, and drinks
9.01	Understanding dangers of water
9.02	Understanding dangers of electricity
9.03	Understanding dangers of heat
9.04	Handwashing before starting
9.05	Assembly of equipment
9.06	Preparation onto tray
9.07	Use of liquid level indicators
9.08	Pouring cold
9.09	Pouring hot
9.10	Spooning from one vessel to another
9.11	Spooning from narrower neck jar
9.12	Measuring using large screen display
9.13	Measuring using talking scales
9.14	Measuring using balance scales
9.15	Measuring using measuring spoons
9.16	Measuring using cup
9.17	Measuring using spoons
9.18	Spreading using knife using spoon
9.19	Using safe knife cutting, e.g., KiddiKutter®
9.20	Using a sharp knife
9.21	Grating

DOI: 10.4324/9781003280132-11

9.22	Peeling
9.23	Wash/scrub veg
9.24	Opening packets of crisps
9.25	Opening drinks bottles
9.26	Opening jars
9.27	Opening packets
9.28	Opening packets of cereal
9.29	Tetra Paks®
9.30	Opening tins with MagiCan opener
9.31	One-Touch opener
9.32	Other preferred opener
9.33	Safe use of kettle with tipper or without tipper
9.34	Travel kettle
9.35	One-cup water heater
9.36	Use of toaster
9.37	Use of talking microwave
9.38	Use of manual microwave
9.39	Use of timers
9.40	Washing up
9.41	Keeping surfaces clean and tidy

10.00	Simple drink or snack meal using appropriate skills
10.01	Cold drinks
10.02-10.04	Hot drinks
10.05 -10.16	Snacks
	All detailed in "Let's cook" in appendices

Prerequisite Skills

Able to follow safety instructions.

Handouts

Tactile marking

Scalds and burns

Preparing for Food Technology in secondary school

Let's cook handouts

Pouring

Using the water heater

Let's cook: Tricks and tips

Food preparation cutting and chopping claw technique

Food preparation cutting and slicing the bridge

Let's cook: Basic skill sheet 1

Let's cook: My skill sheet 2

Let's cook: My skill sheet 3 devices

Let's cook: Hot drink in the microwave

Let's cook: Tuna sweetcorn wrap

Let's cook: Easy pizza

Let's cook: Microwave scrambled eggs

Let's cook: Chocolate mug cake

Let's cook: Microwave baked potato with optional cheese and beans

Let's cook: Flapjack

Let's cook: Cheese and ham toastie

Useful websites and books

Children's Cookbook: Delicious Step-by-Step Recipes

by Katharine Ibbs and Catherine Saunders | 7 Oct 2004

Cooking Step By Step: More than 50 Delicious Recipes for Young Cooks (DK Activities)
by DK Dorling Kindersley | 1 Feb 2018

Cutting using the claw grip: In YouTube, search for "The Claw Grip by British Nutrition:"

https://youtu.be/wVJUD8SSQRA

or "Licence to Cook: Using knife (claw grip):"

https://youtu.be/1PlYOHPTRBQ

Cutting using the bridge method: In YouTube, search for "The Bridge Hold by British Nutrition:"

https://youtu.be/uhNvNMOMBg8

www.howwemontessori.com/how-we-montessori/2019/12/we-road-test-ten-childrens-kitchen
-and-chef-knives.html

https://kiddikutter.com.au/shop/ KiddiKutter® knives manufacturer's site

www.kuhnrikon.co.uk/ Kinder kitchen (dog) knives manufacturer's site

www.inchcalculator.com/convert/gram-to-milliliter/ convert grams to millilitres www.howmany
.wiki/vw/ also converts volume to weight.

www.lakeland.co.uk/search/jar%2Btin%2Band%2Bbottle%2Bopener Lakeland Jar, tin and bottle
openers

This section works through all the food preparation skills that your child will need to access food technology, but they can, and should, be started from an early age and gradually built upon. All the utensils and devices mentioned here, together with suppliers, are listed in the "Suppliers of useful food preparation equipment" in the downloadable eResources. All children love helping in the kitchen and cooking has its own inbuilt reward system.

Begin with simple things that are quick and easy to prepare. Younger children have short attention spans, so simple preparation and rapid cooking are ideal. Some of the inexpensive fairy cake and cookie mixes or Angel Delight mixes available in the supermarkets provide a great activity requiring few skills, no specialist equipment and limited preparation. Let your child do the things he can and support him with the rest. Schools rarely have time to teach all these skills and you often find students are expected to bring prepared and weighed ingredients in for food technology because of time constraints. Don't fall into the trap of preparing everything for your child, as this may be the only opportunity he gets to really learn the skills he needs. Take the opportunity to build in kitchen safety skills as you go along, but most of all have fun in the kitchen.

9.01–9.09 SAFETY IN THE KITCHEN

Clearing and washing up should form part of any cooking activity, but water safety is important in its own right. In theory the hot water tap should be on the left, and cold on the right, but application is inconsistent and not all children know their right from their left.

Mark up the cold tap. How you mark it will depend on what sort of taps you have. Alternatives can include elastic bands or pipe cleaners round the tap, or if you have a single lever put a Bumpon or **Tacti-Mark**™ to indicate the side which will run cold. See the handout on "Tactile marking and labelling" on pages 149–150.

Water from the cold tap should always be used for cooking and drinking, and there is no reason hands can't be washed in cold water, as long as soap use is effective.

Wash hands before undertaking any food preparation. It should be perceived as part of the whole task. Water and electricity do not mix, so after using water, make sure your child understands to dry his hands immediately, regardless of what he is moving on to do.

Introduce any electrical devices cold and disconnected from the mains. Explain how they work in principle, before ever connecting to the power. Help your child develop a healthy respect for the dangers of electricity, as just by curling fingers too far round the plug and onto the prongs it is easy to create a circuit as the plug is inserted into the socket. You can buy or make a manipulation board, complete with a disconnected socket to enable your child to practise safely, before progressing to a switched live socket. Inserting and removing plugs requires both dexterity and hand strength. If your child struggles, look out for easy pull plugs with handles. These reduce the risk of curling fingers round to the prongs and also reduce the force needed to remove the plug from the socket. Electricity is a difficult concept for many children and safety largely relies on them believing that what the adult says is true.

By this point your child may well already understand hot and cold but take every opportunity to introduce him to relative levels of heat and the specific dangers of hot. He will also need to understand the different risks of dry and wet burns or scalding. This may require controlled exposure to higher temperatures under supervision and at a safe distance. A child with little or no vision cannot see heat, so is dependent on safe practice and sensing the rising warmth. Using a toaster can be a good way of learning more about heat. As it heats up you can help your child safely feel the heat rising and the process is reinforced by the smell of the toast cooking. The toast is also relatively hot when it pops up but cools quickly to be safely handled.

Whatever task your child is undertaking, encourage him to assemble all equipment onto and work on a tray. If possible, use a tray that contrasts with the surface you are working on and any utensils or dishes you are using on the tray. The tray keeps everything contained, making it easier to find, but also reduces the risks of slipping and burns from anything spilled. If you wish, the tray can be used instead of a plate or double as a chopping board. Look for trays with high sides, and if possible, rubber feet to stop them sliding.

Ensure your child is competent pouring cold, before allowing him to move on to hot liquid. Encourage the use of a liquid level indicator, even when pouring cold, to reduce the risk of your child accidently using his fingers when pouring hot. Tactile jugs cannot be read safely when measuring hot liquids. Remember the severity of burns is determined not only by the temperature of the liquid, but also the percentage of the body covered. Younger children burn more easily at lower temperatures and the same amount of liquid affects more of their body. Teach your child what to do if he does burn himself, as immediate action can make all the difference. Find out more about pouring in "Let's cook: Pouring" on pages 198–200. This also includes information of using travel kettles, kettle tipper, and the One Cup water heater (9.33–9.35).

9.10–9.17 WEIGHING AND MEASURING

There are plenty of talking and large display scales on the market at a reasonable price. Choose scales that will zero between additions of ingredients and preferably one that will toggle between grams and millilitres. This then allows you to measure liquids more easily instead of using a separate tactile or talking measuring jug. If it doesn't toggle, you can still measure liquids, as for liquids like water and milk the weight in grams is almost exactly equivalent to the volume in millilitres. It is more complex for more viscous liquids like oil, but these are usually used in small amounts that can be measured easily with measuring spoons. If you prefer to calculate it out, there is a handy online guide that allows you to convert a variety of liquid measurements into grams. www.inchcalculator.com/convert/gram-to-milliliter/

Encourage your child to spoon ingredients from the packaging into the bowl of the scales. Pouring it in can result in a sudden tip, allowing far too much to fall in, and if you are adding on top of other ingredients, it can be very difficult to be sure which ingredients you are removing.

For some children spooning from one vessel to another can be difficult. Deep bowl spoons keep the food more securely on the spoon and it is a good idea to practise with foods that stick to the spoon better. To maximise independence when making drinks for instance, consider adding sugar from a sugar tipper. This works well for coffee too.

9.18–9.23 SPREADING, CUTTING, SLICING, AND GRATING

Make life easier for your child by having the right tools for each job. This includes utensils that are specifically purposed for each task and also the right size for your child's hand.

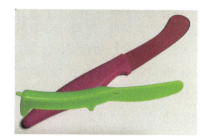

You can buy knives with a broad rounded blade that are ideal for spreading and they are even better if there is a degree of flexibility in the knife. Look for butter knives, that tend to be shorter and rounded and are great for small hands or try sandwich knives that combine a wide blade for spreading and a serrated edge for cutting the sandwich in half. If your child is unsuccessful spreading with a knife, try using the back of a spoon. Fresh bread can roll when spreading, so start your child off learning to spread on cold toast. Butter spread, rather than butter, also spreads more easily. If you want something more visible, try chocolate spread.

A blunt knife is more dangerous than a sharp one as it will not gain sufficient purchase on the food and may slip. If you are anxious about your child using sharp knives look for products designed specifically for teaching children. There is a huge range of devices specifically designed to protect small hands and there are also blade-resistant gloves. In the image alongside we have a plastic knife that cuts through vegetables and salad, like lettuce and cabbage easily, the Kuhn Rikkon dog knife with a serrated edge that cuts through most things and the Pampered Chef® child safety knife. The best child knives are sharp enough to cut through when used in the correct sawing motion but will not cut the hand. The Kuhn Rikon and the KiddiKutter knives are exceptionally good for small hands and links to the products are in the useful websites above.

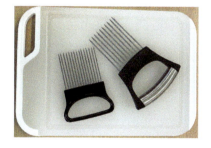

Teach your child how to hold knives safely and the correct techniques for cutting safely. See the food preparation handouts on page 206 and page 208 for teaching the bridge and claw techniques. Good techniques will protect the fingers, but if you child still struggles, or you remain anxious, there are several different finger guards on the market that help with knife placement and keep little fingers safe. Type finger guard cooking into a search engine or onto Amazon to find many different examples. The onion holders are worthwhile investment, as the keep fingers safely away and hold the food in place and can be used to guide the knife.

As your child becomes more proficient with handling knives you can move onto adult knives. Look for ones with bright contrasting handles. There are many around now with brightly coloured blades too. If you can, choose blades and handles that contrast with the chopping board and the food being cut. Schools and food establishments are required to have chopping boards designated to food types. So, in school you will see vegetables cut on green boards, meat on red boards, and fish on white boards. These provide no contrast for children with vision impairments. There is no reason you can't use different colours as long as they have designated uses. You can buy a range of different colours or you can buy white boards with different coloured trims. The ones with silicone or rubber edges hold their position better. You can add Tacti-Mark™ or cut notches into the board so you can differentiate between them.

You also find that schools tend to use tower graters. Whilst these are inexpensive and effective, they do not contain what is being grated. The oval bowl graters are easy to use, and the integral bowl keeps the food contained ready to use. These are also inexpensive and widely available. It is also possible to buy plastic holders for the food being grated, to stop the fingers and nails getting too close to the grater. Look for food safety holders or a mandolin food holder. Rotary graters are another safer alternative for CYPVI since hands don't come into contact with the blades. Food goes into the top and the child turns the handle in either direction, (in some models you need to turn the drum round) making them suitable for right or left-handed users.

Your child may be expected to undertake some skills like grating and peeling for food technology, but these are not always essential for personal food preparation. For instance, a grated cheese sandwich is much more difficult to eat than sliced cheese sandwich for someone with reduced vision. You can slice cheese really thinly using a cheese wire or a cheese slice. Many vegetables do not really need peeling either and a good wash with a vegetable brush or glove will suffice, leaving more roughage and more of the nutrients in the vegetable. If your child is going to use a peeler, try several different types to see which he finds easiest. Those with small hands may find the Palm Peeler helpful. Show him where the blade is and stress the need to keep his fingers away. It is very easy to get nasty cuts from peeler blades. Teach him to try and be systematic and go round the same way each time. It is possible to feel where has been peeled as the surface texture changes.

9.24–9.32 OPENING

Opening packages requires hand strength and control. Your child will need to master crisps and drinks packaging if he is having a packed lunch at school. Fizzy drinks, whilst ever popular with children, are difficult to open. The can or bottle has to be kept upright, whilst at the same time either lifting the ring pull or twisting the lid. Getting small fingers under the ring pull is difficult, but the rings on canned drinks are usually too small to use a ring pull lifter to get greater leverage. Bottled drinks also require a great deal of finger strength and a good firm grip. Using a small piece of Dycem™ can help and this also works with jars. There are some good devices that fit under the kitchen cupboards that reduce the need for the two hands working in opposite directions.

If your child struggles to pull and tear packages open, teach him how to open packaging with scissors. Good kitchen scissors can be invaluable, as not only can you open packets, but you can use them to cut food up. Sliced meats for instance cut beautifully with scissors. If you don't want to use knife to slice pizza up, you can use scissors for that too, although a rolling pizza cutter that sits in the palm of the hand does a great job too.

Investigate how many different types of Tetra Pak® your local supermarket carries. There are so many different ways of opening them, and unfortunately, being able to open one type does not mean you will be able to open others. The most challenging tend to be packs where the corner needs to be torn off (here again use kitchen scissors) and the ones that after you unscrew the top have another smaller plastic ring to pull inside. These are really difficult to get hold of and pull.

If you are looking to buy a tin opener, consider the Culinaire MagiCan™. They are simple to lock onto the tin and have a very positive click in the right place, are suitable for right or left-handed users and come in several different colours. Some people are concerned because they take the whole lid off, but the edge is usually quite smooth, and it keeps the lid attached until you open it into the bin. If you teach your child to approach the opened tin from the base, there is little risk of cutting themselves. It takes time to teach a child with severe sight impairment to open tins. Tinned peas are usually the cheapest thing to buy to practise on. It is possible if you tape the open end *very* carefully to reuse the other end for practice. However, the resistance is not the same without the contents in the tin and this is not a recommendation. If your child cannot manage a manual tin opener, then the best option is a Culinare One Touch™. Although the design has changed a couple of times, the principle remains the same. They are easy to site correctly on the tin, remove the lid neatly with one touch and hold the lid onto the opener until you reach the bin. If you are opening tins where the food is surrounded by liquid, it is worth purchasing a tin lid strainer to remove the unwanted liquid without losing the food.

There are plenty of jar and bottle openers on the market and many different types of tin openers. Ask your Habilitation Specialist if they carry a range that they can let you try before you buy new ones for home.

9.33–9.40 SMALL ELECTRICAL APPLIANCES

There are many small electrical devices that make food preparation and cooking simpler and easier for CYPVI but beware of cluttering the work surfaces with devices that are used only occasionally. Your child needs as much clear surface as possible to be safe in the kitchen.

You will need an appliance to heat water, whether it is a kettle, travel kettle or a one cup water heater. There is more information on hot pouring above and in the "Pouring" handout on pages 198–200. The next most important device is a toaster, which allows CYPVI to prepare warm simple snacks in relative safety. Choose a cool wall toaster and as always, allow your child to explore it while cold and disconnected from the mains. Mark significant heat levels with Bumpons or Tacti-Mark™ and give your child nonconductive tongs to lift the toast out. Tongs give confidence to those anxious about the heat from the toaster.

While your child is still learning you can use a microwave as a safer alternative to the hob or oven to give him greater independence with a range of snacks. The new talking microwave from the RNIB is delightfully simple to use, with just three buttons, one for power, one for minutes and one for seconds. However, this still comes with a hefty price tag of over £200 before VAT. Most people never use all the fancy programmes, but more complex talking microwaves are available from Cobolt systems and the RNIB. For most families the cost of these devices means that children and young people need to learn how to use the family microwave. Avoid complex electronic controls and choose a microwave with simple controls, preferably a dial for power and another dial for time. Almost all microwaves have a one-touch control for quick heating and cooking, usually a one minute or quick cook button. You can adapt the use of the microwave to use this button only if other controls are proving inaccessible. Any controls you use can then be marked up with Bumpons or Tacti-Mark™ to make them accessible. Use an accessible timer, like a phone or Alexa, to give more accurate timings than can be obtained on the dial. With a little practice your child will be able to cook a range of basic drinks and snacks.

If your child is really taken with cooking at home and wants to progress, investigate steamers for fish, potatoes, and vegetables, slow cookers for simple one-pot cooking and using a George Forman grill in place of the oven grill. These can all be made accessible by timing cooking supported by the use of separate accessible timers.

Let's cook: Simple snacks and drinks

10.05	Cereal with milk
10.06	Toast
10.07	Beans on toast
10.08	Sandwiches
10.09	Scrambled egg
10.10	Omelette
10.11	Baked potato
	With cheese filling
	With beans
	Other fillings
10.12	Pizza
10.13	Soup

Now it's time to start cooking.

There are several downloadable recipes/orders of work in the appendices and a range of tricks and tips to make it easier. There are also checklists in the online documentation so you can record progress.

The easiest place to start is with breakfast on a day you are not in a hurry to get out for school. Cereals and toast are relatively simple and can be washed down with fruit juice, rather than a hot drink to start. As you move on, choose activities that will build his skills, so include chopping or slicing and practise until he is competent.

Build on this by preparing food that will be enjoyable for him to eat but will still build his food preparation skills. Include pre-prepared products like mug cakes and fairy cakes that are quick and easy or make milkshakes and smoothies that all still develop skills, before moving on to creating full recipes together. Rice Krispie cakes also require no cooking, but develop spooning, weighing, and mixing skills, as well as potentially learning how to open packaging.

Fruit salad can be made with any fruit in season. You can vary the difficulty by using hard or soft fruit and make just an individual pot or a family dish. It will help your child develop skills in peeling, chopping, and slicing fruit as well as pouring. If you cover the fruit with juice from a Tetra Pak®, you will have incorporated yet another skill.

If your child is heating soup through, most table crockery will struggle to take a full can of soup. Heat soup through in a large jug and pour into the bowl for eating. There is then less risk of spillage in the microwave and when you remove it from the oven the handle removes the hand a bit further away from the heat and gives something secure to grip.

Try recipes yourself first and adapt them to be accessible to your child. Consider where decisions are made visually about whether something is cooked or not and replace it with clear guidelines on power, temperature, and cooking time that work with your cooker or devices. Timings will vary from one device to another.

11: Household chores

11.00	**Household chores**
11.01	Washing up
11.02	Wipe surfaces
11.03	Drying up
11.04	Tidy own toys/things
11.05	Laying the table
11.06	Dust
11.07	Vacuum
11.08	Sweep inside or out
11.09	Make own bed
11.10	Change bedding
11.11	Dirty clothes in washing basket
11.12	Help with washing
11.13	Make own drinks
11.14	Make own snacks

DOI: 10.4324/9781003280132-12

Activities to work on these skills

My chores sheet

Prerequisite skills

Fine and gross motor skills

Handouts

Household chores for children and young people with vision impairment by approximate age

Changing the bed

Useful websites and books

In YouTube, search for: How does a blind girl wash the dishes?

https://youtu.be/OARhOZKV7KE

In YouTube, search for: How does a blind person make their bed?

https://youtu.be/YcFWILxGCvY

In YouTube, search for: How to fold short sleeve shirts with the flip fold:

https://youtu.be/doOi_54AcE0

Young children love nothing more than to mimic the activities of parents and carers. Tasks that adults find boring and mundane appear exciting and very grown up to children. As adults you can trade on that fascination and develop understanding, skills, and systematic approaches from an early age. It doesn't need to be structured. If your child shows interest and it is safe, then let your child help. It starts with toddlers being given a pan and a wooden spoon to feel involved in the kitchen, which in turn starts the understanding of household tasks and cooking.

The chores that your child can achieve will depend very much on her size, her age, and the stage she is at. The suggestions below are just that – suggestions. It is up to you to ensure your

child is safe at all times. However, there is a handout in the appendices on pages 186–188 which gives suggestions for chores based on approximate ages, but remember age is less important than your child's developmental stage.

Your child may show an interest in a particular area that you can broaden and develop. There is little more absorbing than a brush in the yard. Add some leaves or some water and the entertainment level rises exponentially. It's fun, but at the same time the child is learning how to wield a brush and how to sweep. If you can provide child-sized equipment, so much the better. Once she is out in the garden, she may like to water the flowers or even start her own little gardening area.

11.01–11.03 WASHING UP, WIPING DOWN, AND DRYING

Children seem to love messing in water, so learning about washing the dishes is a great place to start. Don't have the water too hot to start and be prepared to rewash anything your child cleans! If necessary, put your child on a step stool in front of you so she can reach the sink. Start with unbreakable items and gradually progress onto crockery as she becomes more adept. Withhold glassware and sharp knives and the like until your child has more understanding and is generally more proficient. Use a bowl or mat where possible to reduce clunking against the sink. As your child matures and develops greater skills, you can raise the water temperature or get her to add her own washing up liquid. You can pour a dollop of liquid into the hand to regulate volume or put it into a pump soap dispenser that will give a controlled amount. Don't let your child just pour washing up liquid into the bowl! Your child will be able to feel if there is anything stuck to the dishes with her fingers. Just like your hair, clean dishes will squeak. Your child will have more control and gain more feedback without gloves.

Progression is to extend the items your child washes. Help her learn which items need washing in what order. Glasses need clean, hot water, but are slippery, so need considerable dexterity. Broken glass presents a considerable risk to younger children. Sharp items should only be washed by children who are proficient and follow instructions. Keep dirty knives in a tub or container or laid across the back of the sink. The child must understand where the blade is and be able to wipe the knife from the handle to the point, away from the bladed side. Knives should then be put to dry, securely, point down where the hand will not brush the blade.

Stacking dishes on a drainer is another skill. Always make sure there is enough space to prevent dishes tumbling down and, at least early on, completely clear the drainer before you start. The adult can take on the drying role initially and ensure items are removed fast enough to leave adequate space. It may be that you swap roles, and the child dries as you wash, or you supervise them completing the entire task, but with fewer items. Every child is different in terms of their vision impairment, cognition, and prior relevant knowledge (**PRK**), so you will need to personalise delivery for each child. As a matter of course all surfaces should be wiped down and any lying water removed.

11.04 TIDYING UP

As a basic precept, a child with a vision impairment needs to understand, if you get it out – you put it back … If you don't put it back, you may not be able to find it again. It is the earliest introduction to a systematic approach, that is so vital to future success. Start with putting toys or their own possessions away and build on it, but remember, in order to be able to do this successfully, everything needs its own home. Incentivise the task by awarding stars, marbles, whatever works! See the sections on "Advanced dressing and organisational skills" for more ideas.

If you have a family pet, maybe she could start taking responsibility for feeding it or grooming it. Many CYPVI now have access to buddy dogs from Guide Dogs and taking responsibility for care and exercise is one of the aims, so that it prepares youngsters to be good future guide dog owners.

11.05 THE TABLE

Your child can also help at mealtimes by laying or clearing the table. Choose the tasks that are most suitable to the age and ability of the child. Start off by perhaps asking her to set out the placemats or put the beakers on the table. Don't give her your best dinner service or the crystal glassware to start off! She could even start just putting her own tableware out. At the end of the meal, she can remove the placemats and coasters and wipe the table down. As she grows and becomes more competent, she can place the cutlery. This is made easier if you can keep the cutlery in systematic trays. It then provides an opportunity to talk about what goes where and how each utensil is used.

11.06–11.11 CLEANING

Cleaning is never the same fun when you have to do it, so try and keep it light and fun. Dusting is easy as long as surfaces are clear, but if not, your child will need a substantial amount of control to avoid knocking items down. It is even more difficult if you use aerosol surface sprays, as these are difficult for CYPVI to target safely. Probably not a task for the youngest helpers!

Vacuuming can also be a good activity, providing your floor is clear of anything that might damage the vacuum. Upright vacuums are generally easier for youngsters to control as there is less likelihood of waving hoses causing damage or sucking inappropriate things up. Pick a large clear area to start and be prepared to supervise closely. You may prefer your child to sweep and if you are concerned about sweeping indoors, let her loose outside with a yard brush. Brushing leaves is great fun and she is unlikely to cause any damage outside. Cleaning the windows outside with water spray and a cloth also appears to be entertaining. The windows will need cleaning afterwards, but the basic principles are acquired.

As an extension of the general tidying role, you may like your child to straighten her bed each day. This can be started from a very early age. Show her how to pull the sheet taut and tuck it underneath, then she can plump the pillows up and ensure the bedding covers the mattress.

Changing the bedding is another level of difficulty entirely. Your child will need to be reasonably tall and have a good reach before being able to do this successfully. See the handout on "Changing the bed" on pages 184–185 before you introduce this and take a look at Lucy Edwards' YouTube video, *How Does a Blind Person Change their Bed*, if you want to use the burrito method.

11.12–11.13 WASHING

There is no suggestion that your child should be taking full responsibility for washing, but it can be great fun to help and builds a great understanding of what needs doing in the future. Make sure there is a washing basket easily accessible and that she knows once clothes are dirty, they go in there. It is the beginning of the washing process, but also an introduction to the idea that she should wear clean clothes and make sure dirty ones get washed.

Once you have a load ready you can talk about sorting into light and dark and how some clothes needing to be washed gently, but it is just preparatory work. If she is really interested, show her how you can use apps or a colour reader to find out what colour clothes are and determine which wash cycle they should go on. She can also help by identifying the different textures of material going into the washing machine. However, she will enjoy putting the clothes into the drum for you, checking how full it is, and when it's ready, turning it on.

If you have a dishwasher, she can help with loading that too, but be careful of sharp knives or forks pointing up out of the cutlery container.

If she is going to help on a regular basis, you may think it worthwhile getting the washing machine marked up. The easiest way is just to put a bumpon against the programme you use most often and if the start button is not obvious, something on there too. If your controls are more complex you may want to use Tacti-Mark™ which offers a finer line and more flexibility. If she can reach, she may like to help pegging washing on the line which develops

her hand strength as well as teaching her the next stage in the procedure. Once everything is dry, she may be able to help pair socks up. If her vision is very low, she may not be able to manage to match them, but she should be able to fold them and roll the tops down to keep pairs together. You can wash and dry socks with sock locks or sock snaps on, which keeps the pairs together. If you put them into a wash bag it even further reduces the risk of them getting pulled apart. She will probably also enjoy folding flannels, towels, or tea towels. Start with small items that need just a simple fold and then progress to more complex items. You can make it easier by purchasing or making a flip fold device like the one in this YouTube video. https://youtu.be/doOi_54AcE0. (In YouTube, search for: How to fold short sleeve shirts with the flip fold.)

11.4–11.5 DRINKS AND SNACKS

By now, the older child should no longer be relying on you for every drink and snack. Revisit pouring if she struggles. Make sure that you keep drinks like squash and milk in smaller bottles as the big two litre ones are very heavy for smaller hands. If possible, keep everything set up in the kitchen for her, with a tray and a liquid level indicator if she needs one. If it is not all just there it becomes too much trouble and an excuse not to make the attempt. Make sure she can identify the cold tap and turn it on and off, preferably without splashing water everywhere. If she has moved onto fizzy drinks, whilst more expensive, you may want to consider small bottles or cans, as the two litre bottles, whilst more cost effective, are heavy and easy to spill. Fizzy drinks are notoriously difficult to pour because they fizz up easily.

There is a whole range of simple snacks you can try with your child in the "Food preparation and snacks" section. Breakfast is a great place to start as cereals or toast are relatively quick and easy.

There is a "My chores" sheet on pages 131–132 if you want to get your child involved in choosing which tasks she undertakes. You can convert this into a reward chart if you feel she needs incentives to join in.

12: Transitions

12.00	Transition
12.01	Home school liaison
12.02	Orient self in new setting
12.03	Locate toilets
12.04	Locate dining
12.05	Strategic classrooms
12.06	Significant people
12.07	Access dining systems and electronic payment
12.08	Appropriate social interaction at breaks
12.09	Uniform
12.10	Safety

DOI: 10.4324/9781003280132-13

Activities to work on these skills

Activities from all the previous sections will support a successful transition

Handouts

Tips for transition to secondary school for parents and carers

Preparing for Food Technology in secondary school

Online: Tips for transition to secondary for receiving schools

Online: Parent questionnaire transition to Year 7

Useful websites and books

Go Big. The secondary school survival guide Matthew Burton, Wren and Rook 2020

Written in a child-friendly format to allay the fears of students transferring to secondary school.

Thomas Pocklington guidance on getting ready for secondary school:

www.pocklington-trust.org.uk/student-support/secondary-school/six-steps-for-getting-ready-to
-start-secondary-school/

BBC bitesize information on starting secondary school:

www.bbc.co.uk/bitesize/tags/zh4wy9q/starting-secondary-school/1

www.bbc.co.uk/bitesize/articles/znncpg8 preparing your child for secondary school.

Resources for schools supporting students through transition to secondary school:

www.youngminds.org.uk/professional/resources/supporting-school-transitions/

Transition is a daunting word. It implies change, either of state or location. Most people dislike change, and particularly major change. In her book, *Between*, Sarah Ockwell-Smith asserts that "Tweens … need to navigate one of the biggest, and according to research, most stressful life events: the transition to secondary school".[1]

How much more difficult must such a transition be for CYP with vision impairments, without the ability to recognise new faces, or create visual memories of the new setting. Yet within the span of this book some children may have had to undertake this major transition twice.

---

1   Coelho, A & Romao, M. Stress in Portuguese middle school transition: a multilevel analysis. Spanish Journal of Psychology 2016 19 (61)

For some children there will be a transition from infants to juniors. This might be just a departmental move, or it could be to a whole new building in a completely new school. The transition to secondary is much more significant. Not only does the building change, there are new staff, friends may have gone elsewhere, and a whole new way of working is introduced. The levels of personal responsibility also ramp up.

Our children spend an enormous amount of time at school. For many children it is not the joyous experience one might like, but there is much that can be done to improve matters.

Allegedly we spend 15% of our childhood at school, but for young children it will feel like much more as it is a greater proportion of the life they have lived. In term time they spend more waking hours in school than doing anything else.

Given that children between 6 and 13 need between 9 and 11 hours sleep, and they are required to spend around 7 hours a day in school, the chances are there will be only 6 or 7 hours available to them to spend time with family or engaging in leisure activities in the week. Some of this time will be committed to specific tasks, like travelling to and from school, washing, dressing, eating and increasingly, homework as they progress through school. No wonder children get tired.

All students will be anxious about the change, will be afraid of getting lost and fear not making new friends. Whilst a vision impairment will make some of these tasks more difficult, the issues are not insurmountable.

First of all, reassure your child that anxiety before moving to secondary school is normal and use the parent transition questionnaire to establish how ready your child actually is to move on to a new setting. You can then use the results to decide which areas you need to address.

Basic school systems

See if you can arrange extra visits to the school beforehand and try and take advantage of any summer school activities the school may run. These are often less formal and introduce children to staff and the setting, as well as allowing pupils to start creating friendships. If you do not already have a **Habilitation Specialist** involved, contact them for an assessment. They may be able to offer input to familiarise your child with the layout of the new school and, where appropriate, work on the route to and from school.

Look online at the school website and see if the school has produced a virtual video tour of school and play this through with your child. The school may also have produced an information or transition pack which gives more information on how the school runs, uniforms, important staff, and may include a map. Your **Habilitation Specialist** or **QTVI** can get it enlarged or can arrange for a tactile version if necessary. If there is no transition pack in place, speak to the specialists who support your child, to see if they have produced something. Communication and Autism teams, as well as **Habilitation Specialists** and **Vision Support Teams** often provide something along these lines.

Compare the size of the school with primary school. Explain the difference between primary and secondary schools, the way the bells ring to tell pupils move from lesson to lesson. If you have older children at the school, encourage them to talk to your vision impaired child about how the school works on a day-to-day basis and allay as many fears as possible.

Reassure your child that *everyone* will be in the same boat, not knowing their way around!

12.01 HOME–SCHOOL LIAISON

Good communication is key to a successful transition.

If your child has an **EHCP** make sure that the **SENCo**, or equivalent, takes part in the transition review meeting. Make sure you voice any concerns and give the school an opportunity to address them before your child starts.

Share information about your child's vision impairment and any other conditions and point out the implications for the school. Establish who your child should speak to if they have concerns or issues at school. This might be a mentor, form teacher or head of year, depending on the school's pastoral system.

If you feel it would be helpful, ask if your child can have additional transition days at the school.

Make sure school knows how your child will get to and from school. If your child has an **EHCP/ CSP** or equivalent, he may be eligible for home–school transport. If so, this is usually free to eligible pupils of statutory school age. Your school, **QTVI** or **Habilitation Specialist** may be able to help you apply for transport. As an alternative you may be offered a bus pass for your child.

Sanctions and detentions: Schools have different policies on sanctions and rewards. Special schools rarely use after school detentions as many children are transported to and from school and it would be a logistical nightmare. However, many mainstream schools use afternoon detentions as a matter of course, sometimes even expecting pupils to serve detention on the same day. It would not be unreasonable to require notice of any detentions, to allow you the opportunity to make alternative arrangements for your child's journey home if, for instance, the child normally used a school bus that did not run later, had a vision impairment that impacted more in low light, or needed to travel in the company of a supportive friend or sibling to keep them safe. This is a reasonable adjustment.

12.02–12.06 ORIENTATION

If necessary, your **Habilitation Specialist** should be able to familiarise your child with the layout of the school and identify any potential problem areas.

Check that the child can get safely and independently to the entrance, from the entrance to an agreed point, usually either a form room or a resource hub. Toilets and the dining area are also important as well as being able to find that significant person, designated to support your child in the event of a problem.

In some new builds, toilets are open plan access, and it can be difficult to determine whether they are designated as boys or girls. It is important that the child is comfortable locating and using these toilets. If not, request that they have access to a disabled toilet that is easier to locate and navigate round independently. Any steps should be well lit and have either ridges leading in and/or a highlighted step.

If the child cannot travel independently around the building, consider other options. They may be able to travel independently after mobility input, but what is being put in place in the interim? If it is that the pupil struggles with the sheer volume of traffic in the corridors, can he have permission to leave lessons five minutes early? Are they just a little anxious and would providing a buddy system build confidence moving round? Or is he simply not able to undertake the route and needs staff support to move round?

12.07 DINING SYSTEMS

Find out how the school dining system works. It is usually a canteen system that offers a much wider choice than generally available in primary schools. Making choices from a large menu may present difficulties, and when offered a wide choice it becomes easy to spend more than anticipated. Menus are usually cyclical over a few weeks and varied by terms or seasons. The school should be able to get you copies of the menu so you can help your child make informed choices.

Payment can be another area of concern. It might be a fingerprint or card system or in some cases, cash. Schools often avoid cash to reduce potential bullying or dinner money being used for other things. Some systems require you load money online, and others pupils have to put cash into a machine and then pay via a fingerprint. If your child needs to pay by cash, or load cash into a machine, check he knows how to identify all UK coins and notes. Can he calculate the cost of his meal and ensure there is enough credit to cover it? If not, you will need to practise these skills over the summer.

The other problem with a canteen system is that pupils usually load food onto their trays and carry it round the canteen to their table. This is not a skill people tend to practise at home. Can your child carry a tray? If not, practise at home. Get a high-sided tray and start with a plastic or melamine plate that won't break if it falls. For food add some marshmallows that will roll, but not too quickly, and practise moving round keeping the tray level. If they can get across the room without spilling, they can eat them! You can gradually move on to things that roll more easily.

If you are thinking you will avoid these issues by sending a lunch box, check if your child can open their drink or insert a straw independently? Can he open his crisp packet or remove the lid off a flask independently? There is usually less dinner time support at secondary school, but also your child will want to be as independent as possible and not appear different from his peers. Practise opening the lunch box and make sure he is familiar with the packaging and opening of all the food that might be in his lunchbox. You may like to develop this further and prepare your child for food technology. This would include opening tins and packets and weighing and measuring, all of which is covered in more detail in the "Food preparation" section.

12.08 SOCIAL SKILLS

Teach your child to repeat the name of anyone they are introduced to in a short phrase, for instance, "Nice to meet you, *Tom*". This makes the name more memorable and also affords the other person the chance to correct their name if your child has misheard.

The lower your child's vision, the more difficult he will find it to locate friends in the playground. Some schools use separate playgrounds for different year groups, to reduce the numbers of children milling around. Other schools also create quiet, or "no ball game" areas to make socialising easier and may have a designated "meet-up" area or friendship stop.

If the school runs any lunch clubs, encourage your child to join. These provide great structure over lunchtime and the chance to meet and make new friends. Don't worry if your child does not make lots of friends initially. These things take time. The activities in the "Social skills" section will help your child develop confidence.

12.09 UNIFORM

You will be required to label clothing for school. Whilst print name labels are welcomed by staff, it is a nice touch to also label clothing in such a way that your child can recognise their own things. This can be problematic, particularly if your child has sensory issues, but can provide other benefits.

A small button that sits inside the collar at the back of the neck, not only identifies a sweatshirt, but helps indicate it is the right way round. You can do the same in the waistband of a skirt, to ensure it is the right way round.

As an alternative you can sew Braille-like bumps onto labels using French knots.

Ensure the uniform is correct and that the child can dress and undress for PE. Refer back to "Advanced dressing skills" for further guidance.

✓ **Practise dressing in the new school uniform before the big day. You don't want to suddenly discover difficulties at the start of term**

✓ If buttonholes are stiff, see if you can replace the buttons with slightly smaller ones so they slide through more easily

✓ Many schools require a more formal, polishable shoe, with no branding. If your child has only worn trainers until now, make sure the shoes are broken in beforehand and the child is able to adapt their walking style to accommodate shoes

12.10 SAFETY

Walking to school

If your child is going to be walking to school on their own for the first time, practise, practise, practise the route with them.

✓ Walk beside them initially, pointing out landmarks and the safest places to cross

✓ Always use controlled crossings (pelicans and zebras) if they are available. Then drop further and further back until you are confident that they know the route and are crossing roads safely. Your **Habilitation Specialist** can suggest the safest route for your child, which may not necessarily be the most direct

Catching the bus to school

If your child will be catching the bus to school, practise the route with them and ensure that they know how to check bus numbers, pay or scan their pass, and know where to get off.

✓ The world has changed since the advent of Covid and although at the time of writing restrictions have been relaxed, it is worth going over strategies in case they are reinstated. Children with reduced vision may struggle with social distancing, so you need to talk to them about how to do this as much as they can in a relatively confined space

✓ If your child has useful vision, get them to select a seat with the best view of landmarks. This will vary from bus to bus, but quite often these will be those seats designated for disabled or older people. Choose a view out of the front or towards the front, closest to the pavement, so the side view is not restricted by other traffic

✓ Encourage your child to ask the driver to tell them when they get to their stop, but don't rely on this. The bus app Moovit is really good as you can program it with a route, and it will beep when the right bus is approaching and also beep when they are coming up for their stop

✓ A bus pass avoids the need to carry exact change. Your child may qualify for a concession travel pass or a local authority bus pass. Many bus companies also have systems to allow contactless card payments. (See Section 6 "Money skills" on pages 56–61 for more information on money handling and payment cards.) Investigate which options are available to your child on the bus routes he will travel. Make sure he knows where the pass has to go and rehearse the names of the stops and saying them out loud to the driver

✓ Provide a back-up way of paying for bus fare in the event of the pass getting lost. The standard fare, or the amount for a child's daysaver taped in the bottom of the bag in an envelope works well as an emergency procedure.

Mobile phones

If your child is walking to and from school or catching the bus independently, they should have a mobile phone. They should know how to use it, have emergency and school numbers programmed in, but also know an emergency number off by heart in case they lose their phone. If possible, choose a mid-range phone that doesn't make them a target for either thieves or bullies. Your old phone if you upgrade is perfect. If your child needs the accessibility of Apple products, the oldest version still on the market will do everything they need at this stage.

Personal safety

Does your child know your home address and area of the town/city?

Do they know what to do if they get lost? It might be worth running through some "what if" questions with your child and clarify that they have some idea of what a sensible thing to do would be:

✓ *What if you see a fight on the way home?*

✓ *What if you lose your phone?*

✓ *What if you get lost?*

✓ *What if you miss your stop on the bus?*

✓ *What if you lose your dinner money?*

✓ *What if you can't find your classroom?*

Part 3

Appendices

Appendix 1
Activities

Activity 1
Making an emergency call activity

Explain to the child you are going to be watching/listening to a boy making an emergency call. If your child is concerned reassure him that the boy is an actor. Ask your child to listen and see if he can answer the following questions after the video.

What is happening?

What number does the boy dial?

What information does he give to the operator?

What does the operator tell the boy to do?

Play the video at the following link, or search in YouTube for "The Correct Way to Make an Emergency 999 Call from DWFireRescue:" https://youtu.be/fTb_jCnbutk

This is a demonstration of the correct way to make an emergency call, produced by Dorset Fire and Rescue. You can play this again if necessary.

Does the operator offer to do anything that you might think is strange?

The usual advice in a fire will be **get out**, **stay out**, **call the fire service out**, but here the operator offers to stay on the phone. According to Dorset Fire and Rescue who made this video, this film is aimed at children who could be frightened, so the operator would offer to stay on the phone for reassurance. They would offer them safety guidance to ensure they are not in a dangerous location and away from smoke. If they are unable to leave the property, the operator would automatically remain on the line passing fire survival guidance until the arrival of the fire engine.

Have a go to take it in turns to pretend to be the operator and the person making the call. Reinforce the script that the operator will use, so your child is familiar with it, and make sure he can answer all the questions including recognising terms like service, incident and address. Ensure your child can give the address clearly in a standard format. This scenario is based on being in a house with a fire and using a landline to call. Try creating different scenarios to call the other emergency services. Use an old or disconnected phone for the child to practise dialling the number.

Because of the prevalence of US programmes on the television many children believe the emergency number is 911.

Emergency numbers in the UK are **999** and **112**.

Activity 2

My fire evacuation plan

We have a smoke alarm at home ☐

We have tested the smoke alarm and listened to the noise ☐

If the smoke alarm goes off, if possible, I must get out of the building and go to ☐

_____

I know the number to call the Fire Service ☐

_____ or _____

My fire evacuation plan

My escape route from my bedroom

My escape route from other rooms

Activity 3

Emergency!

Emergency!

Your house is on fire. Who will you call?

_____

What number will you dial?

_____ or _____

What will the operator ask you?

Activity 4
Using a pelican crossing

✓ Find the pelican crossing using clues like the tactile pavement or the lights and sounds

✓ Locate the pelican button

✓ Stop at the kerb

✓ Press the button

✓ Look and listen

✓ Wait for the beep or the spinning tactile unit (until the WAIT sign goes out)

✓ Cross the road

✓ Keep looking and listening while crossing

Press the button

Which is the Wait Sign? Which is the Cross Sign? Colour them in.

Activity 5

iPhone skills checklist

Name

SKILL	DATES AND NOTES					
Turn phone on						
Connect charger						
Access Siri request information						
Use Siri to send simple message						
Use Siri to make a call						
Turn VoiceOver on using Siri						
Activate voiceover using triple click						
Voiceover gestures						
Swipe right/left						
Swipe up/down						
Tap 1/2 fingers						
Tap 3/4 fingers						
Select app						
Add contact						
Access display accommodations						
Change text size						
Zoom						
Magnifier						
Photo zoom						
Use apps						
be my eyes						
Bus checker						
Email						

SKILL	DATES AND NOTES					
Google Maps						
WhatsApp						
Kindle						
Clew						
Moovit						
Seeing AI						
Soundscape						
Tap TapSee						
NaviLens						
Text message						
Twitter						
Contract management						
Pay as you go top-up						

Activity 6

Tying a necktie

USING THE FOUR-IN-HAND KNOT

Lift the collar up.

Wrap the tie round the neck with the wider end to the favoured hand. The thinner end should reach to about the waist. If you have useful vision, stand in front of a mirror. All manipulation takes place just below around the sternum. Hold the tie part way up the length, not near the end unless you are pulling through.

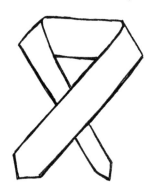

1. In the area towards the collar, now make a cross by crossing the thicker side over the thinner end.

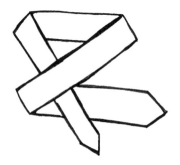

2. Now tuck the thicker end under the thinner one.

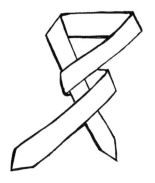

3. Then flip it back over in front of the thinner end.

Tying a necktie

USING THE FOUR-IN-HAND KNOT

4. Whilst holding the tie loosely, push the thicker end up towards your neck with the other hand, behind all the material and the knot that is starting to form.

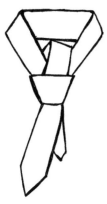

5. You can now make a tunnel through the front loop where the tie made the cross over. Push the thicker end of the tie, down through the tunnel, so the thick and thin ends lie on top of one another.

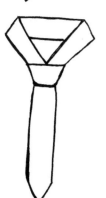

6. Grip the knot with one hand and hold the thinner end with the other and slide the knot up closer to the top button.

7. Flip the collar back down.

There are some good videos on YouTube to help.

Easily tie a four-in-hand necktie knot:

https://youtu.be/w0bObp6loaU

How to tie a tie – 3 simple necktie knots easy to tie (no description but very clear visuals):

https://youtu.be/jKYTVxoaMQA

Activity 7

How to wash your hair

YOU WILL NEED:

Hot/warm water in a bath, shower, or wash basin

Shampoo

Conditioner

A towel

Jug to pour water/shampoo eye shield (optional)

Gather all the equipment you will need.

Completely soak all your hair with water.

The amount of shampoo you need depends on the length and volume of your hair. If you are using a pump dispenser, try one press for short hair or two for long hair. Otherwise pour a blob about the size of a penny into your hand for short hair and the same again for long. Rub into your hands and then massage into the scalp.

If you are using a shampoo bar, wet your hands and rub the bar to create a lather on your hands, which you can massage into your scalp.

Use clawed fingertips to massage shampoo thoroughly into all areas of the scalp and hair.

Rinse your hair until the bubbles all disappear. You can rinse under the shower, by dipping your head into the water, or by pouring water from a jug.

If you pinch your hair between your fingers and slide along, your hair will squeak if it is clean.

If you wish you can wash your hair again with shampoo, repeating the process above.

Next, put one or two dollops of conditioner on your hand, depending on the length of your hair. Start smoothing conditioner into the tips and length of your hair, before rubbing into the scalp. If you are using a conditioner bar, you will need to wet it and create a foam, before rubbing it into your hair.

You may choose to comb your hair through to make it extra smooth while the conditioner is still in. Leave your conditioner in for two minutes before rinsing it out. The water should have no suds in it. Some conditioners are designed to stay in your hair, so check the product beforehand.

Try and squeeze excess moisture out.

Lean forwards over the shower, bath, or wash basin, put the towel over your head and wrap it round your hair tightly. Stand up and pat and scrunch your hair through the towel until it stops dripping or is towel dry.

Style your hair whilst slightly damp.

Activity 8

Personal hygiene: daily washing

Good personal hygiene is important for both health and social reasons. It entails keeping hands, head, and body clean to stop the spread of germs and illness. Sweating increases during puberty and the bacteria on the body causes it to smell. Personal hygiene benefits personal health and impacts the lives of those around you, too. Looking dirty or smelling bad will not help make friends and increases potential for bullying.

Ensure the child can actually identify the name and location of the body parts.

Some parts of the body produce more sweat – underarms, genitals, and feet and others are on display – face, hands, and teeth.

Parts of the body that need cleaning daily using soap and water.

Face
Teeth
Underarms
Hands
Genitals
Feet

Label the body parts on the diagram or if preferred, a doll can be used to identify the body parts.

Talk through and practise how to wash the face and revisit "Good handwashing techniques."

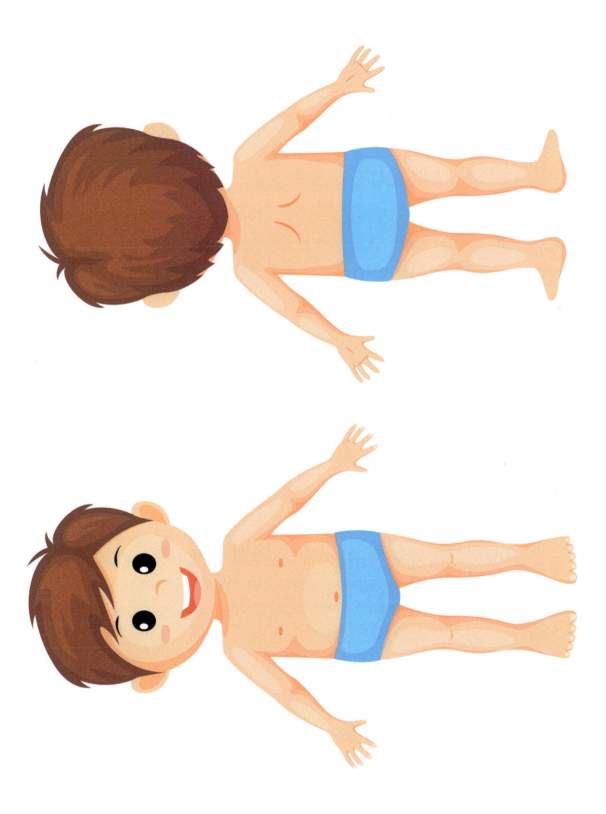

Activity 9

My Lego® teeth

You will need:

A small Lego® base

Enough bricks to create a set of teeth round the base

Play dough

A toothbrush (or brushes)

Toothpaste

Dental floss

INSTRUCTIONS:

You can build you Lego® teeth together, or allow free rein, but decide your teaching objective before starting.

If you only want to concentrate on cleaning teeth – one layer of bricks will do. If you want to convey an understanding that baby teeth are replaced by adult teeth, you may like two layers, but don't forget to stress once they have gone, they do not grow again.

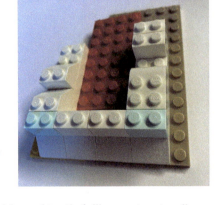

BUILD YOUR TEETH!

If your child has useful vision you may like to choose white bricks for teeth and perhaps exchange some that may be decaying for different coloured bricks. If it makes it more fun, the teeth can be any colour you like!

Build and take apart as many times as you like to convey the idea of teeth falling out naturally or having to be removed by the dentist. You can use the Lego remover tool to differentiate between processes

GET THE TEETH DIRTY!

Smear the teeth with play dough to represent plaque and bacteria in the mouth. If your child has useful vision, you can use dry wipe markers instead if you prefer.

FLOSS BETWEEN THE TEETH

Yes, dental floss will go between Lego® bricks! And it will help loosen the play dough.

BRUSH THE TEETH CLEAN

Use an old brush rather than the child's own and brush the teeth from every angle. The brush alone will probably remove the play dough, but adding toothpaste affords the chance to discuss how effective it is. Talk about brushing in gentle circles to remove the plaque and bacteria without damaging the teeth. Turn the brush to different angles to get to the inside of the teeth and across the top.

Take the opportunity to demonstrate a range of different brushes if you have them and to experiment with different toothpastes, smells and flavours. Your child may be more receptive in a play situation, than when being pressured to clean their own teeth.

Activity 10

All about me

Talking about yourself is not always easy. Let's think about information you may want to share with someone you meet. Jot your answers down.

Your name

Your age

Your hobbies

Any sports activities

Your favourite television show

Favourite music or band

Can you think of anything else?

How do we turn this into a conversation rather than a list? See the first example.

Hello, my name is . . . .

What's your name?

Now go through your list again and write **at least** two sentences or phrases. Your aim is to create a conversation. This requires two people to talk. Try and make the other person feel comfortable. Include things that are current that may spark a discussion. For example:

I love Coronation Street. Did you see it last night? Wasn't it terrible that the house caught fire?

I love playing football. Did you watch the match last night?

Using the information you have prepared, but not reading it, start a conversation. Take it in turns to introduce the topics. Share information about yourself and find out something about the other person. See how long you can keep the conversation going.

Activity 11

Conversation starters: 25 things to say

What do you say in a social situation when it all goes quiet? Rehearse these conversation starters so you can call on them when necessary.

You will need to have a range of options, as not all will be appropriate in all situations.

Don't forget to introduce yourself by name, and if the other person doesn't offer their name – ask what it is. Remember a conversation is two-way. You can't just ask one question then expect the other person to keep talking.

1. So, why are you here today?

2. What do you want to be when you grow up/leave school/college?

3. What are you studying at school/college?

4. If you could be anywhere right now, where would you be? What would you be doing?

5. What's your favourite song? Why do you like it?

6. Can you play a musical instrument?

7. What's your favourite sport/game to play?

8. What do you like to do at the weekend?

9. Have you been to the cinema recently? What did you see?

10. Tell me about your favourite movie or TV show.

11. Do you like reading? If you could only keep one book, which one would you keep? Why?

12. What's your favourite book?

13. What was the last book you read?

14. What's your favourite food?

15. What is the best surprise you ever had?

16. What is the best thing that ever happened to you?

17. What are you thinking about right now?

18. Do you have a pet? If you could have any animal for a pet, which one would you choose?

19. If you could be any animal, what would you be and why?

20. If you could go anywhere in the world, where would you go?

21. What is the nicest thing someone has done for you?

22. What superhero would you want to be and why?

23. If you were stranded on a desert island, what three things would you want to take with you?

24. If you could make three wishes, what would they be?

25. What would you do with a million pounds?

Activity 12

Hello, goodbye, and interruptions

Activity guidance

There are many social situations that can be difficult for students with vision impairments. It is important to be able to recognise whether they are in a formal or informal situation, how they should respond to that scenario, and what strategies they can best use to communicate and engage with others.

Small group work is ideal as you can add in role play, but this activity will work with an adult and a child.

You can add as a many greetings and scenarios as you wish, taking local dialect, colloquialisms, trends and variations into account. Remember first impressions matter.

Explain the significance of formal and informal situations and discuss most appropriate phrases. Some phrases are a little dated but expected by older people in particular.

Suggestions for greetings. "Alright," "Good morning," "Good afternoon," "Good evening," "Hello," "Hey," "Hi," "Hiya," "How do you do," "Oi Oi," "Whazzup," "Yo," "Yo dude."

Responses to a greeting could be those above, or "Good to see you," "Nice to meet you," etc. This can be a good opportunity to introduce and explain "How do you do."

Discuss how you would take your leave from each of these situations.

Interrupting a conversation is always a difficult skill for children, but it is particularly difficult without access to non-verbal cues. Under normal circumstances you would interrupt by establishing eye contact or waving to distract the speaker so that they come to you. The simplest solution is to come within a reasonable distance and say in a clear voice, "Excuse me," or "I'm sorry to interrupt, but …". Explain that such interruptions should only be for valid reasons. A small wave may also attract the other person's attention.

You can undertake role play for a variety of these situations, particularly if you have a small group of children.

HELLO – GREETINGS

How many different greetings can you come up with? List them here or on a separate sheet.

Then match them to the different situations where they could be used. Some could be used in more than one situation.

GREETING
Hello

SITUATIONS
In the playground with friends
At an interview
With family
A formal situation
An informal situation
Meeting the Mayor
Greeting your teacher
A doctor's appointment
Phoning a friend
Phoning a stranger
Meeting a stranger

Activity 13
Personal space

The term "**personal space**" generally refers to the physical distance between two people in a social, family, or work environment. Personal space can be difficult for CYPVI who may need to be closer than is usually accepted to see the person they are talking to, or because with little or no vision they may not even realise how close they are.

There are four spatial zones:

Intimate space, for immediate family or very close, intimate friends between 0–18" (0–45 cm)

Personal space, more distant family and friends dependent on exact relationship between 18" and 4 ft (45–120 cm)

Social space, acquaintances or those you've just met, 4–12 ft (1.2–3.6 m)

Public space, people you don't know, more than 12 ft (3.6 m). This cannot be applied in busy urban areas likes buses and tubes.

Simple rules are:

Don't touch other people or their things without permission.

Aim to stand more than arm's length, or a cane length away from someone who is not family or a close friend.

To better explain personal space, use a hula hoop around the waist to indicate intimate space. Demonstrate the way you can pull the space in or expand it out to exclude or encompass people. If it works better for the student, you can place the hoop on the floor instead. It is usually being too close, rather than being too far away that creates the problem.

If you have access to a larger hula hoop, demonstrate how the space required ebbs and flows as relationships change. People from one zone or group can move into another.

Alternatively use a long cane. Only intimate or close friends should be within the reach of the cane.

Give specific relevant examples to show when people may be made uncomfortable by unusual proximity, for instance, when drawing cash from an ATM or when tapping the pin in to pay for goods in a store.

Show the student how to hold a long cane and push the tip out gently out along the ground in front to just touch the heels of the person ahead, to maintain appropriate queuing distances.

Discuss what sort of situations make them feel uncomfortable and what they can do about it.

Activity 14

Simple timer games

Why are we doing this? It increases anticipation, makes children more aware of the elapse of time and encourages dexterity, speed, and accuracy.

HOT POTATO

You need a potato, a timer, a small group of children/adults.

The game is simple. Players sit in a circle and pass an item, often a potato, around the circle. The person holding the potato when the timer goes off is eliminated. Agree the length of the timer beforehand. Play continues until only one person remains.

STAR JUMP CHALLENGE

You need space, a timer, one or more children.

How many star jumps can you do in a minute? Try and beat your score the next day. You could count skips over a rope instead if you prefer.

STACK 'EM UP

You need a flat surface, a bowl of coins the same size or denomination (pennies), a timer

How high can you stack your tower without it collapsing in one minute?

You can make this easier using small building blocks or stacking cups or as an alternative you can use cereal hoops or chocolate squares. Paper or plastic cups can work but add an additional challenge because they have to be in a pyramid shape. Use anything that will stack, without actually clicking together.

THE WORD CHALLENGE

You need a way to record your words and a timer.

How many complete words beginning with the letter … (your choice A to Z) can you write before the timer goes off? Remember some letters will be much harder than others. Decide if you will allow proper nouns or products beforehand, if your child can recognise them. Set your timer for 3 minutes – or another agreed time, remember if your child is a Braillist recording words may take longer. If you want to differentiate the game – give different players, different letters.

KEEPY-UPPY

You need space, large balloons, a timer, and a small group of children.

You child may need some useful vision. Choose strong primary-coloured balloons that your child can see best. Who can keep their balloon off the ground for …? Depending on the abilities of the children, start with 30 seconds, rise to a minute, and keep going …

Name ....date..........

Activity 15

Meet Alexa

✓ List 5 things that Alexa can do that you think particularly help people with vision impairments

✓ List 5 things that Alexa can do that you think you would use at home

✓ List 5 things that Alexa can do that you think you could use at school or for homework

Name   date

Activity 16

Money skills

Cut and paste the coins in value order onto a new sheet of paper

Name   date

Activity 17

How many pounds?

Activity 18

Find the prices

Find the prices of these products. Are they the same in a small local store and the big supermarket?

Product	Small shop	Supermarket
A chocolate bar		
A can of coke		
A packet of crisps		
2 litres of milk		
A bunch of grapes		

Is there a way we can save money on shopping?

Activity 19

My chores

Cut out and stick your chosen chores onto the "My chores" sheet. If using print, the sheet can be laminated to make it reusable. Create your own chores on a separate sheet. Rewards are down to personal choice and circumstances. You can use smiley faces, stars, an ice cream, or offer pocket money as a reward.

Wash the dishes
Load the dishwasher
Unload the dishwasher
Lay the table
Make the bed
Put clothes in washing basket
Tidy own room
Dust
Vacuum

My chores

Appendix 2
Handouts

Handout 1

Emergency services handout

In an emergency in the UK you can dial 999 or 112. Calls to the emergency services are free

Abuse of the emergency number is an offence

The operator response is the same regardless of how you connect

Hello, emergency, which service do you require? You can then select the service you require.

You will need to be able to give the location of the emergency – address and telephone number, if necessary, as well as describing the nature of the emergency. It is helpful to rehearse this with role play. The child will need to know their name and understand the term address, as well as being able to give it accurately.

MOBILES

112 also works throughout Europe. Furthermore, the 112 number works across networks, meaning that your phone will try to call 112 using another network at times when your usual network is down, or the signal is poor.

Children often mistakenly think 911, which is the American number, will work in the UK.

You can call the emergency services even if you have no credit or if the mobile is locked.

Access to mobile phones varies from brand to brand. If the child has their own mobile phone, they can be taught to access it, but younger children may not have a personal phone, so may need to be taught how to access a parent's phone.

LANDLINES

On a phone with buttons, like a landline, there is a bump on the number 5.

Decide whether your child can best locate 999 or 112 and practise using the template below which can be raised on a Minolta machine if required.

Not all households have landlines and in the event of a fire the landline may not be accessible. Where possible, teach using a real large-button phone and reduce down to the size of the family phone over time. The child will need to know numbers and their location on the phone.

EMERGENCY SERVICES

Ambulance

Fire

Police

Coastguard/lifeboat

Mountain rescue

Cave rescue

Services on the ground may call for air support, including air ambulance, or air sea rescue.

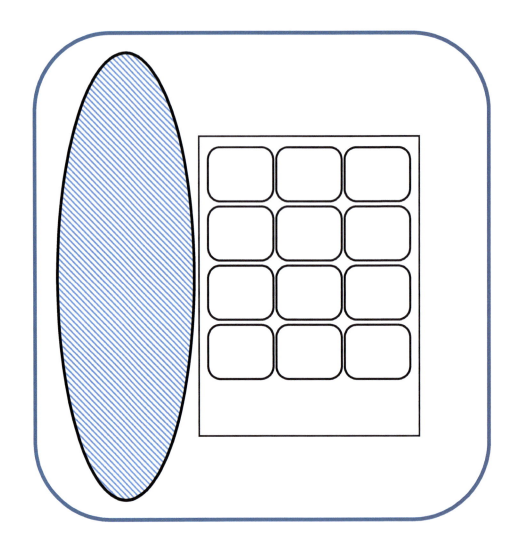

1	2	3	4	5	6	7	8	9	0
⠁	⠂	⠃	⠙	⠑	⠋	⠛	⠓	⠊	⠚

＊   #

Handout 2
My safety rules

✓ Stay away from strangers. Explain what makes a person a stranger. Note that even someone with a familiar face is a stranger if you do not know him or her well. Make sure your child has an understanding of safer strangers, for example, someone in an appropriate uniform, police, paramedic, or a woman with a small child or a buggy.

✓ Stay away from anyone who is following you on foot or in a car. Don't get close to them or feel as though you must answer any questions they ask you.

✓ Run and scream if someone tries to force you to go somewhere with them or tries to push you into a car.

✓ If you can get away, and can see the car, run in the direction opposite to the way the car is facing. The vehicle would have to turn round to come after you, giving you a bit more time.

✓ Set up a secret code word. Tell your child not to go with anyone under any circumstances unless that person also knows this code word.

✓ Agree a coded message for your child to text you or call when out with friends or at a sleepover that will mean, "Pick me up I don't feel comfortable". Ring back with an excuse they can use to leave.

✓ Adults shouldn't ask children for help. For example, a child shouldn't trust grown-ups who ask for directions or for help finding a puppy or kitten. A child who is approached in this way should tell the person, "Wait here and I'll check with my mum or dad," and then find his or her parents right away.

✓ Ask for help when you are lost, stay still, don't just wander. If you get lost in a public place, immediately ask someone who works there for help.

✓ Always ask for permission before going anywhere with anybody. Ask a parent or the grown-up in charge before leaving home or the play area, or before going into someone else's home. Do not accept **any** unplanned offers for a ride – from someone known or unknown.

✓ Always tell a parent or carer where you are going, how you will get there, who is going with you, and when you will be back. Be home at the agreed time or ensure you let your family know.

Handout 3
Apps for staying safe

When you start letting your child go out and about independently you may well be anxious about their safety. There are several apps that allow you to monitor your child's whereabouts and offer additional security. Try different apps to see which suit your family circumstances. A mobile phone is a vital safety tool for children and young people travelling independently. Always ensure the phone is charged, has credit, and has important contact numbers saved in the phone.

Life360: Family Locator and GPS Tracker

Create your own private groups, called "Circles," of family members and chat with them in Family Locator.

View the real-time location of family members on a private family map that's only visible to your Circle.

Receive real-time alerts when family members arrive at or leave destinations. Works on both Android Phones and iPhones. In-app purchases.

Hollie Guard turns your phone into a personal safety device. Protect yourself from violence and accidents, record evidence, and alert emergency contacts of your whereabouts quickly and easily. If you feel like you're at risk, shake your phone or tap the screen to generate an alert. The app will share your location and record audio and video evidence, these details will be sent to your emergency contacts who can take action and get help. Free – iPhone only.

WhatsApp. allows you to stay in touch with your friends and family. End-to-end encrypted group chats let you share messages, photos, videos, and documents across mobile and desktop. Make secure video and voice calls with up to 8 people. Your calls work across mobile devices using your phone's internet service, even on slow connections.

Share your location with only those in your individual or group chat and stop sharing at any time. Works on both Android phones and iPhones. Free.

What3words divides the world into 3 m × 3 m squares and assigns each square 3 words. As opposed to GPS coordinates, the 3 words are meant to be more human-friendly and easy to remember. It is accessible by speech and is often used by the emergency services. It is used to help locate you in an emergency. If your child can't read it, ask them to take a screenshot and send it to a person who can. Free on Apple App Store and Google Play

Remember most phones have inbuilt safety features. You do not need credit to make an emergency call to 999 or 112. Your child may find it easier to locate 112 than 999. 112 will automatically seek out the strongest signal regardless of service provider. Most phones have a way of accessing emergency calls even when locked. iPhone: When the screen is locked keep pressing the power button for the option to call SOS.

Handout 4

Useful apps for travellers

Ariadne GPS: Uses VoiceOver to provide street and route information and offers the opportunity to explore the map of what's around you. Provides information whether travelling on foot, bus, or train. Paid app £4.99 with in-app purchases.

Blind Square: Market leader in navigation GPS for vision impairment. Announces street crossings, junctions, and places of interest. Can search for nearby restaurants or the post office, etc. using voice commands. VoiceOver supported, but includes its own high quality speech synthesis. Paid app £34.99 iOS.

Clew: Student favourite. Clew is a path retracing app designed for blind and visually impaired users to help them independently return to any desired locations. Works indoors in locations such as railway stations, shopping centres schools, or universities. Free on iOS.

Google Maps: Google Maps can now help visually impaired people get to their walking destinations more easily – by reminding them that they're on the right path, warning them when there's a busy junction ahead, telling them how far away their next turn is using voice navigation, and automatically pointing them back in the right direction if they have to stop. Free on Apple App Store and Google Play.

Lazarillo: Lazarillo is a GPS app specifically designed for vision impaired people to explore the world around and set up routes. It announces landmarks as you move around and can continue in the background whilst other apps are in use. The app is free but requires mobile data or Wi-Fi. Available on iPhone App Store and Google Play for Android.

Moovit: Student favourite. Moovit collates train and bus timetables alongside other public data, as well as crowdsourcing information from its users, to provide directions and plan routes. Entering a destination provides a choice of routes, with information on how long the journey is expected to take. It is accessible for speech users. Free on Apple App Store and Google Play.

National Rail: National Rail Enquiries lets you plan, book, and keep up to date with all your train travel in one easy app. Manage your journeys across the Great Britain train network with My Travel, plan new routes with our comprehensive journey planner, and receive real time travel updates. Apple App Store and Google Play.

Microsoft Soundscape: Calls out roads as you pass, advises of junctions coming up and alerts users to shops, post offices, etc. You can also set personal markers for favourite locations. Free on iOS.

UK Bus Checker: Plan journeys, see real time bus information and buy mobile tickets. Supports bus, train tram and underground routes. Free.

What3words: What3words divides the world into 3 m × 3 m squares and assigns each square 3 words. As opposed to GPS coordinates, the 3 words are meant to be more human-friendly and easy to remember. It is accessible by speech and is often used by the emergency services. If you can't read it yourself, take a screenshot and send it to a person who can. Apple App Store and Google Play.

Life360: Family Locator and GPS Tracker. With Life360 you can: Create your own private groups, called "Circles," of family members and chat with them in Family Locator.

View the real-time location of family members on a private family map that's only visible to your Circle.

Receive real-time alerts when family members arrive at or leave destinations,

See the location of stolen or lost phones. Works on both Android Phones and iPhones. In-app purchases.

WhatsApp: Helps you stay in touch with friends and family. End-to-end encrypted group chats let you share messages, photos, videos, and documents across mobile and desktop. Calls work across mobile devices using internet services, even on slow connections.

Share your location with those in your individual or group chat, so they can see where you are with an option to stop sharing at any time. Works on both Android Phones and iPhones. Free.

Be My Eyes: Pairs volunteers with blind or visually impaired people in need of help with small, everyday tasks or recognise landmarks. As it is "real" people, it would not be suitable for children but could prove useful for young adults. Free on Apple App Store and Google Play.

Seeing AI: Student favourite. This app uses the device camera to identify people and objects and then describes those objects using speech. It has different settings and can be set for currency, people, text, and landscapes. Free on Apple only.

Bespecular: Allows visually impaired users to take photos and ask questions about them. It is run by a whole network of volunteers across the globe, but as it is a real person, caution is advised with younger children. Apple App Store and Google Play.

Tap TapSee: A mobile camera app designed specifically for blind and visually impaired users, powered by the CloudSight Image Recognition API. TapTapSee utilises your device's camera and Voiceover functions to take a picture or video of anything and identify it out loud for you. Available free on Apple App Store and Google Play.

Remember apps change all the time and new ones are created. Look on Henshaws Knowledge Village for the most up to date reviews on apps:

https://www.henshaws.org.uk/knowledge-village/

Handout 5
Tying bows and laces

Resources

An apron

Shoelaces, assorted (with aglet)

Ribbons etc.

Directions

BOWS

Practise with ribbons tied round the leg, before moving on to aprons. You can knot two different coloured or textured ribbons together to help your child differentiate between the different strands and can use wired ribbon to help keep the loops in position. Make sure the child can cope with different thicknesses of ribbon. The most common error is to try tying with the fingers towards the ends of the ribbon or laces. Encourage the child to move the fingers closer to the knot.

Remember aprons do not need to be tied behind the back, but can be crossed over at the back and tied at the front.

LACES

Assuming the child already has a basic understand of tying bows, you can move on to shoelaces. Begin with the shoe off the foot, with the heel towards, and the toe facing away from your child. This replicates the position and shaping necessary when the shoe is on the foot.

You may like to fasten two laces of different colours and textures together to help identify which lace is which. If your child has some useful vision, it is often helpful to choose laces that also contrast with the shoe. For children with no useful vision try one rounded and one flat lace.

There is no single way to tie shoelaces; there are a variety of approaches. Each method starts with making an "X" and then a first knot. The way you create the second knot is what varies. Keep the tying method consistent once you have established one that works for your child.

BUNNY EARS OR CHOCOLATE BOX BOW

Using the **bunny ears** method uses the same knot twice. Only move onto the second knot when the first knot is secure.

Make two loops, or bunny ears, and make sure the child holds them close to the first knot and leaves a long tail.

Then cross the loops over and repeat the first knot.

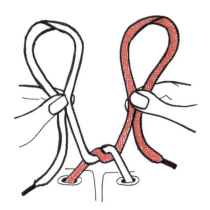

Bunny ears or chocolate box bow.

THE AGLET AND EYELET METHOD

Try this if the child struggles to keep the bunny ears in position. After the first knot is in place, pull the lace out to the side and then push the aglet into the top or first eyelet down. Do the same on the other side. This holds the end of the lace and keeps the loop in position. Squeeze the loop together and repeat the initial knot. Gently tug the aglet out of the eyelet.

BEADS

You can also help your child by slipping a large flat bead over the loops to hold them in place. You can still fasten the knot with the bead in place, although this is only intended as an interim measure.

Using the more traditional single-loop tying, a rhyme or story can help your child remember the steps to shoe tying. One of the best known and simple phrases is "**loop, swoop, and pull**."

Alternatively try:
Make an X.
Pull the top lace through and pull it tight.

Make one loop (holding it tight at the bottom) – this loop is a "tree". The other lace is going to be a "bunny." The "bunny" runs around the "tree" and goes into his "hole." And then you pull the loops tight!

Follow this link to find some videos.

https://theinspiredtreehouse.com/child-development-teaching-kids-how-to-tie-their-shoes/

Things to consider:

If you are demonstrating, or working hand over hand, make sure to have the child sit next to you, or facing forwards in front of you, so they can get used to how the actions feel from the correct perspective. If they sit facing you, they will have to mirror the actions, which is much more difficult.

Children who struggle to control the bunny ears, may benefit from trying with pipe cleaners or wired ribbon first. This helps keep the bunny ear upright.

Handout 6

Open-ended zipper

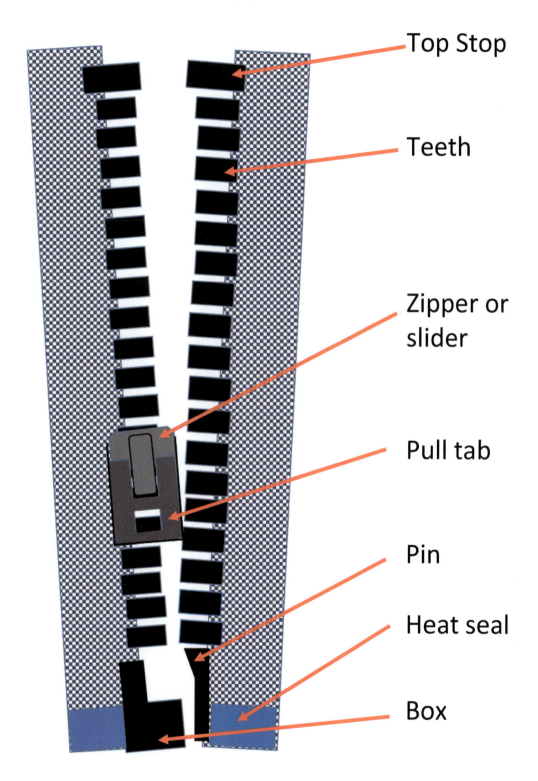

Top Stop

Teeth

Zipper or slider

Pull tab

Pin

Heat seal

Box

Open-ended zips: Always use consistent terminology when describing zips.

If your child has some useful vision, purchase 2 zips in contrasting colours. Split them up and use them so that one colour zip teeth and locator pin inserts into the different coloured retainer box. Where possible get teeth that contrast with the zip tape. Start off with larger chunky zips and gradually get smaller as your child becomes more proficient.

Start with the largest open-ended zips you can obtain. Zips work better when fastened to material, so if you can, just attach enough to make it easier to hold, before moving on to proper garments. Always learn to insert the locator pin with the zip facing outwards from the body, as this will contribute to muscle memory for fastening the item when it is being worn. Don't be tempted to let the child lie the garment down facing them as this be a mirror action and will create a different hand movement.

Ensure the child understands that the locator pin must travel through both the zipper/slider and into the retainer box – with those two pieces joined together in order for the zip to work. One hand must hold the two bits together, whilst the other inserts the pin. This is the most difficult element of the task.

Handout 7
Scalds and burns

95% of all childhood burns and scalds happen at home, but accidents can be prevented if everyone is aware of the risks.

✓ Hot drinks cause most scalds to children under the age of 5. A child's skin is much more sensitive than an adult's and a hot drink can still scald a child 15 minutes after being made. Put hot drinks out of reach of small children and away from the edges of tables and worktops

✓ If your child is using hot water, make sure they are pouring onto a tray, to reduce the risk of hot water running onto their midriff near vital organs. Encourage the use of a coiled flex or a cordless kettle to reduce the risk of accidentally catching the flex or consider using a one-cup water heater

✓ Hot bath water is responsible for the highest number of fatal and severe scalding injuries among young children. Teach children to put in cold water first and then gradually raise the temperature. Never leave young children alone in the bathroom. Ensure your older child knows which is the hot tap and understands the risk of hot water. If possible, restrict your domestic hot water system to 46°C

✓ To avoid pans tipping over, use rear hotplates and turn the panhandles away from the front of the cooker. Practise placing pans securely on the hob – particularly gas hobs and use silicone (heat resistant) pan handles and oven shelf edges that reduce burns and make items more visible for those with some residual vision. Hobs can stay hot enough to burn for some time after use and hands placed on hot hobs will stick. Use oven gloves or potholders that are not worn and are the appropriate size for the child

✓ Microwaves can heat food unevenly and some parts can become very hot. Anything with a high sugar or fat content is particularly dangerous. Always allow food to stand for the required time and use vessels that don't absorb the heat

✓ Children can also suffer burns after contact with open fires, irons, curling tongs and hair straighteners, cigarettes, matches, cigarette lighters and many other hot surfaces. Keep hot irons, curling tongs and hair straighteners out of reach even when cooling down. Remember your child may explore with their hands, so tell your child if there is something hot and where it is

In an emergency make sure your child knows what to do.

Cool the burn with cool or lukewarm running water for 20 minutes as soon as possible after the injury. Never use ice, iced water, or any creams or greasy substances like butter.

www.capt.org.uk/burns-scalds
www.rospa.com/home-safety/advice/accidents-to-children#scalds
www.nhs.uk/conditions/burns-and-scalds/treatment/

Handout 8

Tactile marking and labelling

LABELLING DEVICES AND CONTAINERS

Tacti-Mark™ has a small nozzle ideal for marking the settings on appliances, such as a washing machine, oven or microwave. It can also be used on a variety of surfaces including metal, card, and plastics making it great for adapting games and pictures. It can crack off flexible plastics though. It squirts onto the surface as a thick plastic liquid, which sets to a hard fine line in 24 hours. Once set, it is durable and it is available in either orange or black, only from the RNIB shop.

Bumpons – RNIB offers sets of one single design, or a mixed pack of 80 self-adhesive rubber dots (DL102). They come in several sizes, in clear domes, flat coloured circles, or squares. They are ideal for marking equipment around your home like the functions on your washing machine, buttons on a remote control, home keys on your computer keyboard. They are not as permanent as Tacti-Mark™, but easier to install. As well as the bumps, you can cut out the flat areas to create straight lines to indicate settings more easily. There are also soft touch dots that are great for things like home keys.

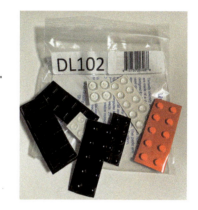

Single designs are also available on Amazon and eBay.

Equipment like cookers and washing machines, that may need multiple markings can use a combination of bumpons and Tacti-Mark.

Labelling clothes

Uniforms can be a particular problem because everyone's clothes look the same. Clothing can be labelled using French knots on the back of clothing or on the label or by using small, shaped buttons. Some people use specially designed buttons, called Slade buttons to differentiate between clothes, but these are no longer easily available. Tacti-Mark™ also works on material so can be used on clothing, but make sure it doesn't come to a point and cause irritation.

RNIB Penfriend audio labelling

Penfriend allows your child to place audible notes on medicine packaging and cosmetics, identify film and music collections, label clothing – washing instructions, colours, coordinating items of clothing and accessories. You can also use it to listen to music or listen to Talking Books:

https://rnibwebappsexternalprod.blob.core.windows.net/ecominstructions/instructions/PenFriend_3_hints_and_tips_(APDF).pdf

NaviLens

NaviLens is a navigation and labelling app especially designed for blind and partially sighted users. It can help navigate and find their way around cities independently, and it can be incorporated into products for easy identification. Users can create their own unique tags for routes or labelling items from their own smartphone. Labels can be read back by pointing the phone in the general direction of the tag. It is free and works on both Apple and Android devices. NaviLens tags are increasingly appearing on Kellogg's cereals.

Find more information on the RNIB website:

www.rnib.org.uk/sight-loss-advice/technology-and-useful-products/technology-resource-hub-latest-facts-tips-and-guides/technology-guides-everyday-living/navilens

Don't forget the basic low-tech tricks you can use to identify things. An elastic band will differentiate between the shampoo and hair conditioner that come in the same bottles. An elastic band or a pipe cleaner will identify your door in a hotel, or the cold tap. If there are products you use regularly – put a bit of sticky Braille on the lid and swap the lids over when you open a new bottle.

Handout 9

Toileting issues

Many CYPVI have issues using the toilet independently. Sometimes it just takes a little longer to master all the skills they need, or there may be one element or task that is just too difficult for them to undertake independently. Some CYPVI can display sensory issues. This can be due to a formal diagnosis of a sensory integration problem or autism, or it can just be because something in the environment overwhelms them in some way. When girls first start their periods, they may need help again in the bathroom, in a way they did not before. This can be resolved in most cases by rehearsing all the necessary procedures over time. If the child is articulate and understands the problem, you can talk it through, otherwise it will be a gradual process of elimination of different strategies to see if you can resolve the problem.

If your child is reluctant to use the bathroom independently consider some of the following areas and strategies:

Understanding

✓ If your child uses objects of reference, make sure you are not sending mixed messages. Don't use a pull-up or nappy to indicate the toilet if you are trying to make him independent. Instead offer the end of a toilet roll or a packet of wipes

Physical difficulties including balance and coordination.

✓ Can he cope with his clothing when he's in a hurry?

✓ Can he physically reach behind himself to wipe, does he understand the movement and processes required? Is his balance good enough to do this? Is he afraid of falling in the toilet?

✓ Can he independently locate the toilet paper or wipes?

✓ Can he tear the paper off the roll or pull a wipe out and is he then dextrous enough to hold it in the best position to wipe?

You may need to move the toilet roll or wipes closer or change the product he uses. If he cannot tear the paper or manipulate it to wipe, you will need to revert back to early hand and finger strength activities. If he can't twist to locate his bottom properly to wipe, try sitting him down and placing something small he really wants on the seat behind him. If he can't get to it immediately, bring it close enough that he can succeed and gradually increase the distance he's got to reach behind him. If he is afraid of falling in the toilet, give him the opportunity to explore the bowl (clean toilet and plastic/rubber gloves!). Show him it is too narrow for him to be sucked through. Does he still need a smaller toilet seat to give him more support?

Auditory

✓ Does he dislike the echoes in the bathroom?

✓ Is he afraid of the flush?

Get him to make his own echo noises in the bathroom, so it becomes a game. Consider gentle music in the bathroom and increasing the softness in the bathroom with a thick bathmat, or more towels. If the flush is the problem, other noise in the room may make it less of an issue, but also consider letting him explore the toilet bowl again. Show him where the water comes from and try and allay his fears.

Olfactory

✓ Does the smell upset him? Some children really can't stand the smells generated in the bathroom

Smell is the most evocative of the senses, if he gets distressed by the smell it may make him even more reluctant to wipe. Try an odour neutraliser or something in the room that emits a scent he likes to mask the others. A scented stress ball may help reduce anxiety when passing motions.

Tactile

✓ Does he dislike the water splashing back up?

✓ Does he dislike the feel of the paper or wipe on his hands?

✓ Does he dislike the feel of the paper or wipe on his bottom?

✓ Is he anxious he may smear poo on his bottom or get it on his hands?

Use a sheet of toilet paper across the surface of the water to prevent water splashing back up. Consider wet wipes instead of toilet paper. There are some that are genuinely flushable and biodegradable, but they tend to be expensive. You can gently warm the wipes, although overwarming will dry them out. There are several commercial wipe warmers on the market.

Maybe consider reusable cloth wipes that are more durable if he worries about his fingers going through the paper. These require a separate clean box and a used box. They are not cheap, so maybe see if you can get a sample or experiment somehow before investing. You can get both terry towel and microfibre ones which are softer on the skin. They have become more common since the various reusable nappies came back to the fore. These are intended for use with cold water but can be used with tepid water if the cold is an issue. They are usually scented with essential oils, so again can provide a masking effect.

If all else fails, maybe try disposable gloves. Children find the loose plastic ones easier to put on than the close-fitting vinyl, latex, or nitrile ones.

If there is a real issue with sensitivity it may be necessary to provide a desensitisation programme. Try and make it age appropriate if possible.

Visual

✓ Is the room too dark?

✓ Does he complain about glare?

For some CYPVI reducing visual clutter in the bathroom may help. If glare is an issue, consider changing the lighting – if it's very bright, turn the main light off and perhaps try individual battery suction lights or mood lights in a colour he likes. Do you have blinds at the window that might give him a little control over the lighting levels?

If he finds it dark, see if the lux levels can be increased, maybe supplement with task lighting in certain parts of the room.

If you are still experiencing problems, an **Occupational Therapist** may be able to help with different ideas. Even with older children, sometimes distraction can work wonders. Keep some games and activities (preferably things that will wipe down) in a basket that you can use to distract your child from the issues that are bothering him. If he requires you to stay in the bathroom with him, Uno or Snap can work well.

Handout 10

Supporting your child with hair washing

Begin early and every time you wash your child's hair, use it as a fun learning opportunity, gradually moving to the point where she can do more and more independently. Allow her to do the bits that she can and support her with the others. Hair will clean at most temperatures, so allow your child to choose the temperature that makes her most comfortable. If she remains resistant, try letting her wash your hair first.

When in the bath or shower, allow your child to pour water with a jug or hold the shower head to get a feel for controlling where the water goes. If using a jug, ensure she understands the location of the spout, and that the water pours best through it. You may need a few old towels round the floor initially to contain any wayward spray!

Demonstrate how to wet her hair and just how much shampoo is right for her length and volume of hair. Get her involved in massaging her scalp and rubbing shampoo through her hair. Using shampoo to stand hair on end is great fun, whilst still helping to clean the hair.

If your child is a reluctant hair washer because of anxiety over getting shampoo in their eyes, consider using "no more tears" shampoo or a shampoo face shield to make it a less distressing experience. These can always be changed later when the child is more confident. Consider products that your child finds attractive, whether visually or because of an attractive scent. The sense of smell is very evocative and scents that children like can predispose them to engage in activities and helps them better remember procedures.

As she gains confidence, give her more responsibility. Ask her to find the shampoo ready and then dispense the correct amount for her hair. Don't over shampoo, it will make it very difficult for your child to rinse the shampoo out. See the suggestion below to help your child identify shampoo and conditioner.

Show her how to lather up the shampoo and spread it across her scalp and throughout her hair. Work from forehead backwards, smoothing the hair away from her face. Use clawed fingers to stimulate and clean the scalp. Work right round into the nape of the neck.

Encourage her to close her eyes and tip her face up towards the ceiling as she rinses the shampoo out and help her learn how to direct the water flow away from her face. This reduces likelihood of shampoo reaching the eyes.

Teach her how to pinch her hair between her fingers and slide the fingers along. If the hair is clean it will squeak.

Repeat the process with conditioner, this time starting from the tips, scrunch the conditioner in and then up the length of the hair, before working into the scalp. Conditioner helps reduce tangles.

Encourage your child to comb her hair though with the conditioner in. As well as spreading conditioner through the hair, it also helps eliminate head lice as they slide out with the comb.

Show your child how to squeeze excess water out of the hair after washing and then, leaning forward over a bath or the shower, throw a towel over her hair and wrap it round. There is a knack to creating a turban around the hair, but practice makes perfect, and clips may help. Discourage rubbing too violently, but instead encourage patting and scrunching to reduce tangling. Aim for towel dry, or slightly damp ready to brush or style hair.

Younger children don't need to wash their hair too often, but sometimes as they move towards teenage years hair becomes greasier. It can be a fine balance between washing just enough and over washing, which stimulates the production of more oil. It may be helpful to introduce your child to dry shampoo, if grease is a major problem.

Use the "How to wash your hair" activity sheet to build in systems and order for your child, so she will eventually be able to undertake the task completely independently. Change anything that doesn't work for her.

Identifying shampoo/conditioner and dispensing/measuring amounts

Choose the ones that work best for you:

✓ Keep only the relevant products on the side of the bath/shelf

✓ Purchase shampoo and conditioner in different shaped identifiable containers

✓ Put a bumpon, Velcro®, or Braille label on the lid and reuse the same lid when the bottle is empty

✓ Put an elastic band or a bobble round one bottle

✓ Create reusable Braille/large print label that fastens on with elastic band

✓ Practise squeezing one blob or two out or comparing volume sizes to something identifiable like 1p or 2p or something else that has meaning to your child

✓ Keep shampoo and conditioner in reusable dispensing pumps. These can be labelled appropriately. Experiment with one pump for short hair and two pumps for long

✓ Consider using shampoo and conditioner bars as an eco-friendly alternative. These can be identified by different scents and eliminate the need for measuring liquids out

Handout 11
Haircare: Brushing

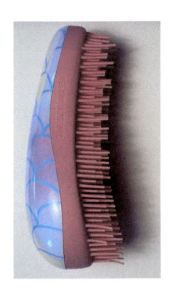

Whether hair is long or short, (unless of course it's a buzz cut all over!) it needs brushing or combing on a regular basis. Choose a brush or a comb that your child can handle and manipulate well. For the very young or those with sensitive scalps, soft baby brushes may be best, but otherwise TangleTeezer™ or other detangler brushes work very well. They fit nicely in the palm of the hand and brush through the hair without too many snags. Make sure your child can recognise the bristles and understands that they need to touch the scalp and run through the hair.

If you are using a more traditional brush, explain the different parts and the functions. A more traditional brush has a handle, and a head where the bristles attach. Adult brushes can have quite long handles, that may make them difficult for small hands. If necessary, get your child to hold the brush higher up the handle, close to the bristles. Be wary of round or thermal brushes (with bristles that go all the way round), as used for blow drying, as without practice, it can be easy to tangle the hair up in these. Also introduce a variety of combs. Combs have teeth as opposed to bristles, but again, you can have a long-handled comb, or tail, or a comb with no tail at all! If your child has afro-Caribbean hair it will be necessary to use an afro comb and you may need alternative hair care strategies.

Work together hand over hand or hand under hand and explain what you are doing. Teach your child to brush from the top of the head, down to the ends of the hair. Be consistent with the language you use. Start from the front, to either side, then do the back. If your child's hair is very long, demonstrate how to pull it forwards over the shoulder and brush it there. Emphasise the need for brushing right into the nape of the neck. Many children just brush the top surface and don't go right through all the hair to the scalp. This can leave a small knot, that over time gets bigger and becomes increasingly difficult to untangle. As your child becomes more confident, transfer more and more responsibility for brushing over to the child. If your child's hair is particularly prone to knots and tangling, try using conditioner or detangling spray.

If you are teaching your child to tie the hair back into a ponytail, use scrunchies, rather than small bobbles to start. These tend to be less resistant to stretching and less likely to ping out of the child's hand. Demonstrate how to put the scrunchie over the fingers and stretch the fingers out wide, so the scrunchie drops across the knuckles. Use the other hand to pull the hair together. Use the hand with the scrunchie to grab the gathered hair, and stretch the scrunchie with the other hand, from the point between the thumb and first finger, keeping hold of the hair and pull it over and through the scrunchie. Hold the scrunchie against the head with the flat of the first hand and with the other, slot the fingers in and twist so the scrunchie sits across the other hand. Now repeat the process with opposing hands to tighten the hold on the hair. The smaller the scrunchie the more dextrous your child will need to be. Let your child practise on your hair, or use a doll or Girls World type styling head to get the hang of it first before trying to tie their own hair up behind their back.

Handout 12

Personal hygiene: Products, tips, and tricks

Many children struggle with personal hygiene for lots of reasons, but there are several products you can switch around to make it easier for your child. Some of these products may evoke sensory issues for the child, so it is a good idea to know of a range of alternatives.

SHAMPOO

If your child is anxious about getting shampoo in her eyes, switch to "no tears" baby shampoo. Alternatively consider a shampoo eye shield.

Transfer shampoo into a pump dispenser to ensure that your child gets a controlled amount of shampoo to wash their hair. You can label a dispenser appropriately for your child with large print or Braille. See the handout about labelling for other ways to identify different products.

Alternatively, you may like to go plastic free and purchase shampoo and conditioner bars. There's no liquid to worry about, just lather the bar up and apply it directly to wet hair.

DEODORANT AND ANTIPERSPIRANT

Aerosol deodorants and antiperspirants are difficult for children and young people with severe sight impairment to direct accurately and for some the dexterity required is just too difficult. Others dislike the noise or the feel of the spray on the skin. Many schools do not encourage aerosols, because of the risks to asthmatics and the general hazards of propellant.

Roll-on deodorant is one alternative. It is easier to apply, but for some the wet feel of the roll-on is just too disturbing. Deodorant/antiperspirant sticks are equally easy to apply and don't feel either cold or wet, so offer a great alternative to the traditional aerosol.

TOOTHPASTE/MOUTHWASH

Cleaning teeth can be particularly challenging for those with oral sensory issues. If you have an extremely reluctant brusher, try and identify if there is a specific issue that can be addressed. The brush alone is quite intrusive, so perhaps consider looking at a smaller toothbrush, maybe even a finger toothbrush if that is all your child can tolerate. Bamboo brushes are available if the feel of plastic is an issue. If your child is a sensory seeker, they may like an electric toothbrush, but others will hate them. If the movement itself is a problem, investigate U-shaped toothbrushes. These are available in electric or manual in a range of sizes and cover all the teeth at once.

Many children and young people simply do not like the taste of mint toothpaste. There is quite a variety of alternative flavours of both toothpaste and mouthwash available, containing little or no mint at all.

TOOTHPASTE	MOUTHWASH
Ecodenta juicy fruit kids	Dentyl Fresh clove and cherry
Berts Bees fruit fusion	Listerine mild berry for kids
Punch and Judy tutti fruiti	Plax natural fresh
Splat natural toothpaste	

Jack and Jill is available in banana, blackcurrant, blueberry, raspberry and strawberry.

Splat oral magic care foam kids. Oral care foams are recommended for use as an additional solution for daily oral care and after each meal or drink when using a toothbrush is difficult or inconvenient.

Remember a gentle toothbrush, and less frequent brushing with mild toothpaste is better than no brushing at all.

Speak to your dentist for advice on unflavoured toothpastes for those sensitive to strong flavours and low foaming pastes.

Oranurse, Jack and Jill offer flavour-free paste.

Your dentist can also refer you on to the NHS specialist dental care services or the Oral Health Foundation may also be able to advise:

https://www.dentalhealth.org/dental-care-for-people-with-special-needs

Handout 13A

Facts about periods

Periods are another name for the menstrual cycle. The cycle can range between 20 and 35 days, but the average is usually 28 days. Initially, the cycle is likely to be irregular, but it should gradually settle down. When you first have periods the time between one period and the next may vary so it can be difficult to know when you will have your next one. When your menstrual cycle becomes more regular you can use a diary or an app to work out when you're due. This record helps you calculate the frequency of your periods and when the next one might be.

Menstruation is really just the result of a girl's body's monthly preparation to create a baby. When a female first becomes able to produce a child, usually between the ages of 9 and 16, it begins preparation once a month for possible motherhood. A tiny egg matures in one of the ovaries, then travels down a fallopian tube towards the uterus. This release is called ovulation. The uterus meanwhile, has been preparing for the egg's arrival, and its lining has thickened to nurture the egg whilst waiting to see if it is fertilised. If the egg is not fertilised, it flushes the egg and the lining out with some blood to clear out ready for the next cycle. This liquid flows out of the vagina as a reddish-brown menstrual flow.

Period blood is often thick and reddish brown and may have small lumps in it. It only smells when it comes into contact with the air.

It is healthy to change your towel or tampon every few hours, which also reduces the risk of seepage or leaking.

You will have to learn how to spot signs and symptoms of impending periods, recognise when blood is flowing and use sanitary products effectively, or know when and how to ask for help.

The idea of losing blood can be frightening, but in fact, although it can feel like a lot, blood loss is minimal with the average being between 30 and 40 ml over the whole period. 30 ml is two tablespoons, or 6 teaspoons of blood. However, the flow can vary from day to day. Periods last between two and seven days, but the average is 5 days. You are therefore looking at losing an average of 6–8 ml of blood a day.

Signs and symptoms

Changes in hormone levels can affect moods.

A woman may feel energetic and sexy around the time she ovulates, or moody, tearful, or angry the week before the period is due. It can help to keep a diary or use a well woman app to see if a pattern emerges. Breasts may become sore or a bit larger and some people may get spots on their face just before the period. Eating lots of fresh fruit and vegetables, having a diet low in sugar and salt and taking regular exercise can help.

Periods may sometimes be painful. Some people get cramps before the period starts, others during. Some women are particularly badly affected. There are medical conditions like PMS that are sometimes associated with periods. Doctors think that as many as three quarters of women who have periods get some signs of PMS.

PMS – Pre-menstrual syndrome

✓ Mood swings. Feeling upset, anxious, or irritable

✓ Tiredness or trouble sleeping

✓ Bloating or tummy pain

✓ Breast tenderness

✓ Headaches

✓ Spotty skin or greasy hair

✓ Changes in appetite and sex drive

There is another very rare condition called **PMDD**.

> Premenstrual dysphoric disorder (PMDD) is a health problem similar to PMS, but it's more serious.

What can you do about pain?

Hold a hot water bottle against your stomach and take a painkiller. The contraceptive combined pill or patch may be helpful for painful periods, but this is only suitable for some and only through the GP. The doctor will be able to prescribe something else. Exercise, such as walking or sport, can help too.

Don't suffer period pains in silence.

Sanitary protection

It's for each individual to decide whether they prefer to use **towels**, **period pants**, **tampons or a mooncup**.

Towels, **pants**, **or pads** are recommended for younger girls. Many schools carry supplies of sanitary products provided to reduce **period poverty**. Keep pads in a zip-up bag to keep them clean or purchase a ready-made **Teen Starter Pack** from Lil-lets. It is available from most chemists and is designed to provide the basics and get girls used to carrying what they need.

You should always bring your own changes where possible, but help may be available in school.

It is a good idea to practise putting pads in place. Most pads have sticky strips on the back to fasten to underwear. It is easy to stick the pad to itself if you rush or haven't practised enough. It takes practice to ensure that the pad sits far enough forward on the pants. It can sometimes help to use pads with wings to ensure the pad sits centrally. Used pads should be folded in on themselves and placed in the disposal bins in the toilets.

Tampons are not usually recommended for girls under 13. Tampons are inserted into the vagina to absorb menstrual flow when people have their periods. They are cylindrical in shape and made of cotton, rayon, or a blend of the two. Tampons are designed to be inserted using a plastic or cardboard applicator or to be directly inserted, without an applicator. **Insertion of internal devices like tampons cannot be supported by school staff** so you must be familiar with your own anatomy and understand the insertion process.

Wash your hands before and after use. Tampons should be changed at least every four hours. Do not try and extend use by using a more absorbent tampon.

Sometimes girls and women can have problems with tampons, leading to a serious illness called toxic shock syndrome (TSS). This is very rare but if you have two or more of the following symptoms while using tampons – being sick, a rash, sore throat, sudden fever, diarrhoea – stop using tampons and see your doctor right away. It is not recommended that you wear tampons for more than eight hours.

Does putting in a tampon for the first time hurt?

No, not if you relax. It can be difficult to put in a tampon if you're tense and not sure how to put it in. When you have your period try putting a tampon in when you have lots of time and privacy. If the tampon feels uncomfortable it may not be in far enough. Read the instructions that come with tampons to find out how to put them in or look online for more detailed instructions and videos.

Mooncup: This is a silicone cup that is worn internally to collect menstrual fluid and can be emptied and re-used.

Young people with sight loss can be naturally anxious about leaking. Practise placing towels correctly at home, as well as in school, and consider back-up solutions for reassurance.

There are special **period pants** that contain leaks, but still feel comfortable. They have additional extra absorbent liners to keep you dry. These can be used in addition to sanitary protection or instead of it. Leading brands of period pants are:

www.shethinx.com

www.wuka.co.uk

www.modibodi.co.uk

Modibodi offers a range specifically designed for teens, and a swimwear range.

You can now find period pants in many major high street stores like Primark and Marks and Spencer.

There is now also a range of reusable towels that can be cost effective after the initial outlay and are helpful to the environment. These fasten in place with poppers.

These reusable products require you to carry a small waterproof bag to store the used products. This can be helpful, regardless of which type of product you use, as sometimes it can be difficult to locate the bins in unfamiliar bathrooms.

One method isn't better than the others. It is entirely personal choice.

The reusable products are more eco-friendly and can work out cheaper in the long run, if you can afford the initial outlay. The most important thing is to use what you are comfortable with.

Personal hygiene is always important, but particularly during periods. You can still bathe and shower. Your vagina is naturally self-cleansing so you don't need to use perfumed pads or special sprays (and these can cause irritation).

Handout 13B

Facts about periods guidance

This is additional guidance to supplement student handout 13A. Choose which content you use depending on the age and ability of the teen. Content in bold is included in the young person's handout. Italics indicate a minor change or expansion of the original. Other content offers guidance. You may find it a helpful way of simplifying information from the FPA 4 Girls leaflet.

> This handout is very loosely based on information in the FPA 4 Girls leaflet:
>
> www.fpa.org.uk/sites/default/files /4girls-female-body-growing-up -puberty.pdf
>
> The leaflet contains a great deal of useful information, but mostly geared towards older teen-agers. The format is quite a busy cartoon design, so not accessible to all CYPVI, but these leaflets are often used in schools.

Periods are another name for the menstrual cycle. The cycle can range between 20 and 35 days, but the average is usually 28 days. Initially the cycle is likely to be irregular, but it should gradually settle down. When you first have periods the time between one period and the next may vary so it can be difficult to know when you will have your next one. When your menstrual cycle becomes more regular you can use a diary or an app to work out when you're due. This record helps you calculate the frequency of your periods and when the next one might be.

Suggest that this is saved in a format that is accessible to the young person and that it is always kept up to date.

Menstruation is really just the result of a girl's body's monthly preparation to create a baby. When a female first becomes able to produce a child, usually between the ages of 9 and 16, it begins preparation once a month for possible motherhood. A tiny egg matures in one of the ovaries, then travels down a fallopian tube towards the uterus. This release is called ovulation. The uterus meanwhile, has been preparing for the egg's arrival, and its lining has thickened to nurture the egg whilst waiting to see if it is fertilised. If the egg is not fertilised, it flushes the egg and the lining out with some blood to clear out ready for the next cycle. This liquid flows out of the vagina as a reddish-brown menstrual flow.

Red cough mixture (clear mixture can be coloured with food colouring if desired) provides a liquid of similar viscosity to blood. Check the terminology is understood as well as the correct names and location of body parts. You can download tactile images to support this conversation from www.rnibbookshare.org/

Period blood is often thick and reddish brown and may have small lumps in it. It only smells when it comes into contact with the air.

It is healthy to change your towel or tampon every few hours, which also reduces the risk of seepage or leaking.

Girls with vision impairments will have to learn to watch for signs and symptoms of impending periods, recognise a blood flow and use sanitary products effectively, or know when and how to ask for help.

Make it clear help can be sought and who from at home and in school.

The idea of losing blood can be frightening, but in fact, although it can feel like a lot, blood loss is minimal with the average being between 30 and 40 ml over the whole period, which is two tablespoons, or 6 teaspoons of blood. However, the flow can vary from day to day. Periods last between two and seven days, but the average is 5 days. You are therefore looking at losing an average of 6–8 ml of blood a day.

Use the red cough mixture to demonstrate flow onto a sanitary towel. Use a 5 ml spoon to demonstrate how little it is. You can also allow a tampon to soak liquid up to demonstrate how it expands. Place it in a glass of water to see just how much it can absorb.

SIGNS AND SYMPTOMS

Changes in hormone levels can affect moods:

A woman may feel energetic and sexy around the time she ovulates, or moody, tearful, or angry the week before the period is due. It can help to keep a diary or use a well woman app to see if a pattern emerges. Breasts may become sore or a bit larger and some people may get spots on their face just before the period. Eating lots of fresh fruit and vegetables, having a diet low in sugar and salt and taking regular exercise can help.

Periods may sometimes be painful. Some people get cramps before the period starts, others during. Some women are particularly badly affected. There are medical conditions like PMS that are sometimes associated with periods. Doctors think that as many as three quarters of women who have periods get some signs of PMS.

PMS – PRE-MENSTRUAL SYNDROME

✓ Mood swings. Feeling upset, anxious, or irritable

✓ Tiredness or trouble sleeping

✓ Bloating or tummy pain

✓ **Breast tenderness**

✓ **Headaches**

✓ **Spotty skin or greasy hair**

✓ **Changes in appetite and sex drive**

There is another very rare condition called PMDD.

> **Premenstrual dysphoric disorder (PMDD) is a health problem similar to PMS, but it's more serious.**

WHAT CAN YOU DO ABOUT PAIN?

Hold a hot water bottle against your stomach and take a painkiller. The contraceptive combined pill or patch may be helpful for painful periods, but this is only suitable for some and only through the GP. The doctor will be able to prescribe something else if it is needed. Exercise, such as walking or sport, can help too.

Don't suffer period pains in silence.

Bring a hot water bottle or microwaveable wheat or lavender heat bag to demonstrate the soothing effect of something warm. If necessary, explain how to fill a hot water bottle safely using a hot tap rather than boiling water.

SANITARY PROTECTION

It's for each individual to decide whether they prefer to use towels, period pants, tampons or a mooncup.

Towels, pants, or pads are recommended for younger girls. Many schools carry supplies of sanitary products provided to reduce period poverty. Keep pads in a zip-up bag to keep them clean or purchase a ready-made **Teen Starter Pack** from Lil-lets. It is available from most chemists and is designed to provide the basics and get girls used to carrying what they need.

You should always bring your own changes where possible, but help may be available in school.

Free supplies are available for schools via **Always**:

https://nationalschoolspartnership.com/sign-up/.

Register for free Always pads and tampons. Always also offer a basic free starter pack to schools that can be given out at the point of explaining the processes or at the first period.

Although teens should always bring their own changes where possible, help and spare products may be available in school. Add specific information here about support available in school. Who to approach for assistance and what products are available.

You may like to look at the following together:

www.lil-lets.co.uk/advice/advice-for-parents

It is a good idea to practise putting pads in place. Most pads have sticky strips on the back to fasten to underwear. It is easy to stick the pad to itself if you rush or haven't practised enough. It takes practice to ensure that the pad sits far enough forward on the pants. It can sometimes help to use pads with wings to ensure the pad sits centrally. Used pads should be folded in on themselves and placed in the disposal bins in the toilets.

Look at the instructions on the pads. Some have different shapes front and back to fit better. Most of the manufacturers have guidance online, which is much more accessible than that on the packs. Practise with clean pants and towels on a surface first and demonstrate where the gusset is and how the pad should lie. Then progress to putting pads into clean pants, but over normal clothing or leggings. Even removing the wrapper can be a challenge to some, so practise that too as well as rolling the towel up for disposal afterwards.

Tampons are not usually recommended for girls under 13. Tampons are inserted into the vagina to absorb menstrual flow when people have their periods. They are cylindrical in shape and made of cotton, rayon, or a blend of the two. Tampons are designed to be inserted using a plastic or cardboard applicator or to be directly inserted, without an applicator. *Insertion of internal devices like tampons cannot be supported by school staff* so the student must be familiar with her own anatomy and understand the insertion process.

Advise the washing of hands before and after use. Tampons should be changed at least every four hours. Do not try and extend use by using a more absorbent tampon.

Sometimes girls and women can have problems with tampons, leading to a serious illness called toxic shock syndrome (TSS). This is very rare but if you have two or more of the following symptoms while using tampons – being sick, a rash, sore throat, sudden fever, diarrhoea – stop using tampons and see your doctor right away. It is not recommended that you wear tampons for more than eight hours.

Does putting in a tampon for the first time hurt?

No, not if you relax. It can be difficult to put in a tampon if you're tense and not sure how to put it in. When you have your period try putting a tampon in when you have lots of time and privacy. If the tampon feels uncomfortable it may not be in far enough. Read the instructions that come with tampons to find out how to put them in or look online for more detailed instructions and videos.

Clear guidance on inserting tampons can be found online – again, much clearer than reading the pack:

https://tampax.co.uk/en-gb/tampax-articles/my-first-tampon/how-to-insert-a-tampon?gclid =EAIaIQobChMIv-Tcx6v66wIVUM3tCh1SyQX4EAAYASAAEgLXnPD_BwE

Mooncup: This is a silicone cup that is worn internally to collect menstrual fluid and can be emptied and re-used.

Information on mooncups is available here: www.mooncup.co.uk/why-mooncup/

Mooncups are now widely available, but you can buy inexpensive unbranded mooncups on eBay for demonstration purposes.

Young people with sight loss can be naturally anxious about leaking. Practise placing towels correctly at home, as well as in school, and consider back-up solutions for reassurance.

There are special period pants that contain leaks, but still feel comfortable. They have additional extra absorbent liners to keep you dry. These can be used in addition to sanitary protection or instead of it. Leading brands of period pants are:

www.shethinx.com
www.wuka.co.uk
www.modibodi.co.uk/

Modibodi offers a range specifically designed for teens and a swimwear range. You can now find period pants in many major high street stores like Primark and Marks and Spencer.

You can buy inexpensive period pants on eBay for demonstration purposes, but the branded versions are much more absorbent and reliable. These eliminate many of the difficulties around getting pads into exactly the right place for CYPVI. They can also provide extra reassurance against leaks when using tampons.

There is now also a range of reusable towels that can be cost effective after the initial outlay, which are also helpful to the environment. These fasten in place with poppers.

These reusable products require you to carry a small waterproof bag to store the used products. This can be helpful, regardless of which type of product you use, as sometimes it can be difficult to locate the bins in unfamiliar bathrooms.

One method isn't better than the others. It is entirely personal choice.

Reusable products are more eco-friendly and can work out cheaper in the long run if families can afford the initial outlay. The reusable pads can be bought by schools through the free sanitary wear in school programmes, but not the pants as yet.

Personal hygiene is always important, but particularly during periods. You can still bathe and shower. Your vagina is naturally self-cleansing so you don't need to use perfumed pads or special sprays (and these can cause irritation).

Handout 14

The puberty pack

Create your own puberty pack to demonstrate to pupils.

Include actual items, not just pictures.

Suggested items – (* items are essential)

ITEM	CHECK
Toilet bag or equivalent*	
Sanitary towels*	
Include panty liners	
Light and maxi pads	
With and without wings	
Tampons*	
With and without applicator	
Mooncup	
Period pants	
Skincare	
Soap bar*	
Liquid soap	
Cleanser	
Toner	
Moisturiser	
Spot cream	
Deodorant – include spray, roll-on, and sticks	
Flannel or scrub*	
Small towel*	

Pick and choose activities to suit the age of the pupil, the time available and your budget.

Shaving goods	
Male disposable razor	
Female disposable razor	
Electric razor	
Gel	
Hair Care	
Shampoo	
Conditioner	
Brush	
Comb	
Hair bobbles	
Teeth	
Toothbrush	
Toothpaste	
Washing up bowl	

A WASHING UP BOWL?

You can carry enough items for a lesson in your bowl and also use it to make the activities feasible in a variety of locations. Demonstrate how everything opens and works. Add in discussions about identifying different products if necessary. For reluctant washers – add crazy or mouldable soap to get them more engaged.

CLEANING TEETH

Toothbrushes – look for own label multipacks and give the brush to the student after the lesson. A four pack in Asda is less than a pound. You can have an old electric toothbrush on hand to show how it vibrates, but not for the student to use.

Alternatively, if the lesson is planned in advance, you can ask the student to bring their own in.

Toothpaste – remember that many students with vision impairment have sensory issues. A number of reluctant teeth brushers dislike the taste of strong minty toothpaste. Children's toothpastes come in a variety of flavours, including various fruits and bubble-gum. Whilst small children's toothpaste may be milder, it is better to encourage brushing rather than impose a flavour that makes students reluctant to brush. There is also an unflavoured toothpaste for those who struggle with the taste.

If you have access to a large set of teeth, you can colour teeth with washable pen or stick tactile debris in to explain about food getting trapped. Remember to explain how other people will be able to see this food, so even if you can't brush your teeth, rinse round your mouth with water after eating.

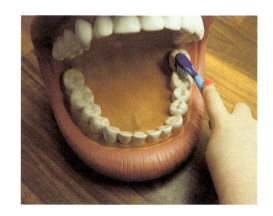

It is also easier to indicate or demonstrate the circular brushing motion on the large teeth.

Activity suitable from primary upwards.

HAIR CARE

Brushing and combing hair: Students may have little or no experience of brushing or combing their own hair. Those with very short hair don't consider it necessary, and those with lustrous locks tend to get a parent to do it.

Brushing requires considerable dexterity and strength as well as a willingness to potentially work through discomfort and pain if it tangles. Parents often find it quicker and easier to just do their child's hair each day.

With a reluctant brusher invest in a TangleTeezer™ – or unbranded equivalent, or suggest parents purchase one and send it in. Soft brushes may seem like a reasonable compromise, but rarely travel through thick hair. Combs with a long broad handle are easier to understand and use than a traditional pocket comb.

Students can practise brushing and putting a bobble in a doll's hair, before practising on their own hair. Bobbles also require dexterity and strength.

Students with afro-Caribbean hair will need showing how to use afro combs and specialist oils and moisturisers for their hair. TangleTeezer also produce a brush specifically for afro hair.

Activity suitable from top primary upwards.

Handout 15

Let's play ...

Board and table games provide opportunities for children and young people to interact more naturally whilst enabling the adult to model good social skills and moderate behaviour. It provides an unorchestrated role play scenario.

Early games suitable for youngsters with vision impairments may include:

Snakes and Ladders, Pop-up Pirate, Simon Game, Crocodile Dentist, and Buckaroo.

These all require sharing, turn taking, conversation between participants, and develop the understanding of winning and losing. They do not particularly require strategy and skills other than dexterity.

Connect 4, Draughts (Checkers), Uno, and Happy Families provide the same degree of interaction, but there is an element of choice and strategy that may impinge on relaxed conversation.

Where possible, pair the student with more socially adept classmates, so they can model behaviour on peers, rather than adults. Encourage appropriate interaction, including, "It's my turn," "It's not your turn yet," "It's just a game!" "That's cheating!" and put each in context.

Progress to allowing the pupil to identify and invite other pupils to take part in games sessions and make choices together with peers about which game will be played. This develops negotiation skills and empathy. The bigger the group, the more negotiation will be required, so start small and grow.

You can expand the skillset by introducing learning games that develop social skills further like Socially Speaking or games that have more complex rules to remember and follow.

Handout 16

Four Simple Rules for good social interaction

#1 Meet and greet politely

In the VI world, we tend to spend a great deal of time encouraging other people to "see" the young person with VI and address them directly. We put the onus on others to initiate conversations and start introductions, but **CYPVI** need to be able to do this too.

Greet people appropriately. Say "Hello," "Hi," "Good morning," "How do you do,"[1] "Pleased to meet you," as appropriate.

Simple exchange. A basic conversation should follow introductions. This could be a reflection on the weather, the location, or an exchange of compliments.

A clear ending. You may need to contrive an excuse to depart, so say something like, "I've got to go now." Alternatively, the conversation may have come to an end, so use "Goodbye," "'bye," or refer back to your opening greeting. Don't leave the other person hanging. If they too have a vision impairment, they may not even realise you have gone.

#2 Take turns

Listen to what the other person is saying. Establish eye contact if you can.

Don't interrupt. Wait for an appropriate gap in the conversation. A conversation is an exchange, and you need to take turns to speak. Some turns may be longer than others. If only one person speaks it is not a conversation.

If you need to interrupt – pick your time carefully.

Respond appropriately. This may mean nodding and smiling rather than saying very much.

---

1   **"How do you do"** is defined as a polite greeting used when first introduced to someone in a formal setting. The formal response is to repeat the phrase back. Whilst regarded as outdated, it is still used in business and formal settings and needs to be understood if not actively used.

#3 Pay attention

Show that you are listening.

Use your own body language to convey interest in what is being said. Nod occasionally. Smile at good or happy things and frown at the bad. Establish eye contact if you can.

Listen to the intonation, which tells you more about how the other person feels.

#4 Think

Think about what you do and what you say.

Don't be unnecessarily rude. Apologise if necessary. Follow instructions and directions. Ask for help if necessary.

Don't touch people or things without permission apologise if you collide, even if you think it was the other person's fault.

Recognise personal space. Personal space can be difficult for CYPVI who may need to be closer to see the person they are talking to, or because of little or no vision may not realise how close they are.

Handout 17

Using Alexa

(Other home devices are available!)

An Echo device allows you to use your voice to set your favourite song as your wake alarm or set a sleep timer to play water or rainforest sounds to soothe you to sleep, check the weather, add reminders, check your calendar, and so much more. There are now over 100,000 skills available in the Alexa Skills store. However, you don't always need to specifically enable apps to do basic functions.

Ask Alexa, and she can tell you the day, the date and the time. With just one voice command she will play radio stations or play different types of music, tell you stories, and call approved friends and family (once set up). You can even use her as an intercom between rooms if you have enough devices.

Alexa can tell you what the weather is outside in your local area, so you can choose the most appropriate attire. She can create a shopping list for you or convert measurements like inches to millimetres, ounces to grams, or even calculate exchange rates between currencies. She is a fount of general knowledge and can even help you spell words.

You can also ask Alexa for basic health and first aid advice from the NHS 111 service. Try asking her what to do if you have a headache.

Alexa can also tell jokes or play games like rock, paper, scissors, or Twenty Questions. Ask her for recipes, and if you want to cook it, you can ask her to give you stage by stage instructions as you go through- she can even send you a shopping list.

If you want to add specific skills, the list is of things she can do is endless. Take a look on the Alexa Skills store for some ideas. Remember apps change over time, new ones are added, and old ones disappear. For most skills, simply saying *Alexa, enable [skill name]* will do the trick. Some skills can be set up by following Alexa's voice prompt instructions, others need to be activated via the Alexa app or on Amazon's website. If you want Alexa to control devices in the home (like turn lights on and off using voice instructions) you will need to buy additional hardware.

If you'd like Alexa to read you or the children a story, sing a song or nursery rhyme, there are a host of options. Look at Amazon Storytime, for instance, which generates a random story for children aged 5 to 12. Or alternatively Story Teller lets you ask for a specific genre such as sci-fi, fantasy or "scary." Audible, the subscription audiobook service, lets you play your current read through your Alexa speaker and control it with your voice. Alternatively, you can listen to certain Amazon Kindle books through an Alexa speaker.

Alexa can also access a wide range of podcasts, including Can't See Can Cook and the BBC Sounds app. Try BBC Kids for a range of activities with household names, or add Disney stories for audible stories from Disney and Pixar.

The more you interact with Alexa, the more things you will find that she can do.

Handout 18

Cutlery skills at mealtimes for children with vision impairment

If your child is severely vision impaired, he will find using cutlery difficult because he cannot learn by watching and mimicking others. It is likely you will have to teach each developmental phase of using cutlery. You may need to refer back to other guidance if there are gaps in his skills.

If your child has some useful vision, select plates that have a single solid colour (self-coloured) that contrasts with food and the table. If possible, contrast cutlery with the plate and the table. You can use Dycem, or other non-slip materials to provide contrast and stability. Provide coloured rather than clear glasses, so that they are visible or place them on contrasting coasters or a Dycem cup holder.

Your child should already know how to lay the table so he understands where he might realistically find cutlery to the side of his plate. Even if you do not use knives and forks at home, it is helpful for your child to be able to eat out in a culturally acceptable manner when out and about.

POSTURE

Good posture for eating and wielding cutlery is very important. It helps with breathing, making the transition from plate to mouth more successful, and swallowing and digestion. It also helps convey a good overall impression.

✓ Sit at table with feet firmly supported. If his feet are swinging, he will have difficulty applying the correct downward force. The chair should be at the correct height for the child to gain support from the table, if necessary, with elbows at right angles

✓ The chair should be pushed in as far as possible to support the back and maintain posture

✓ If he is still using a highchair or child seat, ensure that he is supported on his back or use an inflatable chair cushion to get the correct support and height

He should already understand how to locate food on his plate.

GRIP

If your child does not write with a pen, he may struggle to identify his dominant hand. Generally speaking, if your child is right-handed, he would usually use the knife in this right hand and the fork in his left. However, there are variations on this.

✓ Use "pointer" (index) fingers placed on top of cutlery, fingers pointing down towards plate

✓ Select the correct sized cutlery for your child. The longer the tool, the more difficult it is to manipulate successfully

✓ Cutlery should be held with the index finger ("Peter Pointer") placed on top of the cutlery with fingers pointing down towards plate. Kura Care Cutlery has dips for fingers in the correct places and is child-sized

✓ He could choose to hold knife in right hand and fork in left hand initially to cut up all his food at once – he could then put the knife down and swap the fork back into his right hand to spear food. If he were left hand dominant, he would do the reverse of this

✓ He should locate his food and spear it firmly with his fork towards one end. He will need to be able to gauge a bite-sized distance from the edge of the food. Items needing more force, e.g., meat, should be placed closer to the stronger hand and away from the plate edges to avoid the plate tipping

✓ He should then bring the knife up to the tines (prongs) of the fork and slide down until in contact with the food. He can then cut the food with a firm sawing action

✓ The cut item can then be lifted to the mouth. It is important that the food is firmly speared, so that it stays on the fork as he lifts the food to his mouth

Some children may slide their finger down the fork to help locate food. This is acceptable, but the child should not be surreptitiously trying to pick food up with fingers.

Many children will spear a larger piece of food with the fork and then eat it by biting chunks off. This should be discouraged.

If your child is still struggling seek help from your **Habilitation Specialist** or **Occupational Therapist**.

Handout 19

Locating food on a plate

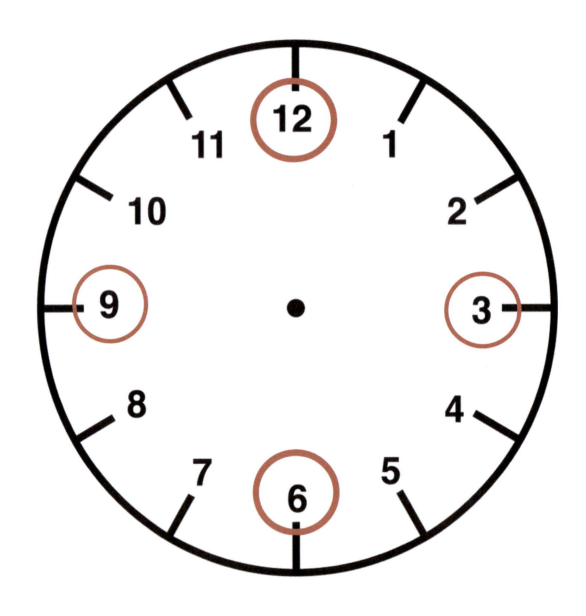

Position of Child

Seated at six facing forward

The analogue clock face is the standard and preferred method of describing the location of food on a plate.

The child needs some understanding of direction, position, and measurement to successfully locate food on a plate.

He needs to understand that there are 12 numbers on the face, where they start and the order. He needs an understanding of half and quarter to make full use of the descriptions you will use. He will need to at least understand where to find 12, 3, 6, and 9. Initially use just, 12, 3, 6, and 9 o'clock.

With the advent of digital clocks, talking clocks and watches, and mobile phones, many children do not understand analogue time. You may need to consider alternative descriptors.

Consider these alternatives:

For 12   top or furthest away

For 6   bottom, or closest to you

For 9   left

For 3   right

If the child does not understand right and left you will have to find alternatives. This could be "closest to me" or in the middle.

State clearly what type of food is where. He will need to practise pushing the fork across the plate to locate his food. This needs to be a controlled movement to avoid pushing food off the plate and to differentiate between different foods. He needs to practice this skill away from the pressure of mealtimes.

Consider always placing the plate so that anything that needs cutting is close to the child, preferably towards the side that he holds his fork. This gives him confidence searching for the food and allows maximum force to be used when cutting. Food should be firmly speared and held in place by the fork, whilst the knife cuts in a sawing motion. Do try and establish which is the child's dominant hand and encourage consistent hand use when using both knife and fork.

Handout 20

Changing the bed

There are several ways you can change a duvet cover, so experiment and find the one that you can describe best to your child and stick with that, unless they really struggle with that method. Changing bedding requires the ability to reach out some distance and work with your arms some way away from you whilst manipulating heavy bedding. It is not suitable for small children and may be something best done together, at least at first. Start with the pillow and make sure it is not over plump for the pillowcase – an old flat pillow is a good starting point. Make sure your child is confident just making the bed before you introduce this and take a look at Lucy Edwards' YouTube video *How does a blind person make their bed?* if you want to use the burrito method.

THE SHEET (FITTED)

Open the sheet so it runs the length of the bed, so you can be sure which way round it goes. On a single bed the length is noticeably greater than the width. Start at the top and lift the mattress enough to hook the elasticated corner underneath. Check the seam is on the corner. Then move to the bottom, pulling the sheet with you along the mattress edge. Lift the mattress and hook the elasticated corner underneath. Check back that the sheet has tucked under the mattress and if not, lift the mattress and pull the sheet under towards the middle. Repeat the procedure on the other side. If the bed is against the wall this becomes much more difficult, as you either need greater reach, or to sit on the bed while lifting the far side.

THE DUVET COVER

1. Inside out
    Lie your duvet on the bed. Turn your duvet cover inside out and reach inside to the two top corners, once you have the corners, use a pincer grip to grab the top corners of the duvet and flip the cover over. You can buy clips to hold the duvet in place while you do this. Hold it up in the air and shake until the cover starts to slide down. Lay it on the bed to pull the cover down and fasten the bottom of the duvet cover.

2. The burrito method
    Take your duvet off the bed. Turn your duvet cover inside out and lie it on the bed with the opening to the bottom (This only works with bottom opening duvet covers.) If you have a preferred pattern, that side needs to be facing down, otherwise you'll have to turn the whole duvet at the end. Lay the duvet on top of the cover, making sure all 4 corners are aligned. From the top of the bed start rolling the duvet and the cover together like a burrito

(or pancake). Your child may find it easiest to sit on the bed to do this. When you reach the foot end with the roll, put your hand through the opening at either end and grab the entire roll and pull it through. Now unroll the covered duvet.

In YouTube, search for "How does a blind person make their bed?"

https://youtu.be/YcFWILxGCvY

3.   The tunnel scrunch

Lie the duvet cover on the bed – right way round this time. Grab the top (narrower side) corners of the duvet and push your hand inside the cover following the seam at the edge until you get to the corner. You can click corner one in place with a peg or clip or keep hold of it while you push corner two into position. The duvet cover will scrunch up as you do this, but if you end up inside the tunnel, it's gone wrong!! Clip the second corner or hold both the duvet and the cover from the outside and shake it down. (You need to be fairly tall.) Lay it on the bed and fasten the bottom up.

Handout 21

Household chores for children and young people with vision impairment by approximate age

Most children love to help in the house, so start involving your child from an early age, as at some point they will rebel. Children who have had an expectation of doing chores at home tend to have a better work ethic and learn about responsibilities.

Household chores are something of a mystery for children with severe vision impairment who cannot learn by copying the actions of parents and carers. Add clear descriptions about what you are doing so that he can visualise the task. There is a hierarchical progression between stages, but the age is less important than your child's ability to succeed.

AGED BETWEEN 2 AND 5	
Put own toys away	Establish a set place for toys and don't move it
Help wash dishes	Do hand wash – even if you have a dishwasher. Start with helping to wash their own dishes, or unbreakable items. Put your child on a safe step in front of you
Help fill up a cat or dog's food bowl	Use a beaker or scoop to help your child measure correct portion size
Help place clothes in the hamper/in the washing machine	Children can be introduced to the idea of washing clothes with tasks they can easily complete
Fold tea towels	Easiest to start with something small and simple
Dust/wipe low surfaces	
Pile up books and magazines on shelves or tables	
Water plants under direction	Using a small watering can
Sweep the yard	Use a child-sized brush if possible
Help wash family car	

AGED BETWEEN 6 AND 9	
Put own possessions away	Establish set places for your child's possessions to encourage him to be systematic. Instil into others not to move his things
Wash unbreakable dishes	Either hand wash unbreakables – (no sharps) or load them into the dishwasher before any sharp items are added
Make own cold drink	Need to be big enough to reach taps and to hold squash bottle securely
Pour own cereal	May need supervision early on and packaging opening beforehand
Fill up a cat or dog's food bowl	
Place own clothes in the hamper or other agreed place	Clothes to be worn again can be placed on a chair
Help load the washing machine	Mark up the washing machine beforehand to enhance understanding and independence
Pair and fold socks	If sufficient useful vision, or work together
Fold simple clothing	Start with towels and get more complex
Dust/wipe surfaces	
Help lay the table	
Clear own dishes from the table	Place on a clear surface or straight into the dishwasher if clear
Water plants under direction	Using a watering can

AGED BETWEEN 9 AND 12	
Put some of own clothes away	Establish set places for your child's clothing to encourage him to be systematic. He may need support with this initially
Wash dishes	Eventually progress to wash dishes independently or load them into the dishwasher before any sharp items are added
Make own cold drink	Use liquid level indicator independently
Pour own cereal or simple breakfast	Including opening packaging
Take responsibility for feeding pet	
Clean pet cage out	

Place own clothes in the hamper or other agreed place	Clothes to be worn again can be placed on a chair
Fold simple clothing	Start with towels and get more complex
Lay the table	
Clear dishes from the table	Place on a clear surface or straight into the dishwasher if clear
Take rubbish to the bin	

AGE 12+	
Put own clothes away	Your child will need adequate space to put away and access his clothes independently
Wash dishes	Either hand wash or load them into the dishwasher including any sharp items. Teach your child to beware handling sharp items or leaving them sticking up in the dishwasher
Make own hot drink	Progress to making drinks for others
Prepare own simple snacks	
Unload dishwasher and put dishes and utensils away	Again, watch out for sharp knives or forks pointing up
Sort washing into colour and dark	You may need a colour indicator or phone app
Load and turn on washing machine	Consider bumpons on your most commonly used programmes
Peg clothes out or hang on airer	
Fold clean clothing	
Vacuum clear areas	
Make own bed	
Help bring in and put groceries away	Explain that different foods go in different locations, teach what goes in the fridge, freezer and the cupboard
Heat own ready meal or snack	

Handout 22

Transition to secondary school

TRANSITION TIPS FOR PARENTS AND CARERS OF VISION IMPAIRED CHILDREN

Reassure your child that anxiety before moving to secondary school is normal.

If possible, arrange extra visits to the school beforehand and try and take advantage of any summer school activities the school may run. These are often less formal and introduce staff and the setting, as well as allowing pupils to start creating friendships. Pupils with more severe vision impairment may also need to visit several times with their Habilitation Specialist to familiarise themselves with the layout.

SCHOOL BUILDINGS AND SYSTEMS

✓ Some schools may be doing virtual video tours of schools and if they do, look at this with your child. They may also send out an information or transition pack which gives more information on school layout. Talk about how big the school is, how it is laid out, and reassure your child that everyone will be in the same boat, not knowing their way around!

✓ Explain the difference between primary and secondary schools, the way the bells ring and pupils move from lesson to lesson.

✓ If you have older children at the school, encourage them to talk to your visually impaired child about how the school works on a day-to-day basis.

✓ If there is no information pack, is there a map or plan of the school that they can give to you? Your **Habilitation Specialist** or **QTVI** can get it enlarged or can arrange for a tactile version if necessary.

✓ How do school lunches operate? Is there a fingerprint or card system and do you load money online or do children put cash into a machine? Can your child identify all UK coins? If not, practise over the summer.

✓ Can your child carry a tray? If not, practise at home with a tray and some marshmallows – they roll but not too quickly! If they can get across the room without spilling, they can eat them! And then move on to things that roll more.

✓ If you are planning on sending a lunch box, can your child open their drink or insert a straw independently?

✓ Can your child pour a drink? If they struggle to see the top of the cup, ask your Habilitation Specialist for a liquid level indicator, which beeps when water is near the top of the cup, and practise!

✓ Ask your **Habilitation Specialist** to assess your child's ability to access food technology at school. Can your child open tins and food packets and measure and weigh?

✓ Practise dressing in new school uniform before the big day.

WALKING TO SCHOOL

If your child is going to be walking to school on their own for the first time, practise, practise, practise the route with them.

✓ Walk beside them initially, pointing out landmarks and the safest places to cross

✓ Always use controlled crossings (pelicans and zebras) if they are available. Then drop further and further back until you are confident that they know the route and are crossing roads safely. Your **Habilitation Specialist** can suggest the safest route for your child, which may not necessarily be the most direct

CATCHING THE BUS TO SCHOOL

If your child will be catching the bus to school, practise the route with them and ensure that they know how to check bus numbers, pay, or scan their pass and know where to get off.

✓ Children with reduced vision may struggle with social distancing, so you need to talk to them about how to do this as much as they can in a relatively confined space should it be required again. Choose a seat with an empty one next to it unless travelling with a companion

✓ Encourage your child to ask the driver to tell them when they get to their stop, but don't rely on this. The bus app Moovit is really good as you can program it with a route, and it will beep when the right bus is approaching and also beep when they are coming up for their stop

MOBILE PHONES

If your child is walking to and from school or catching the bus, they should have a mobile phone. They should know how to use it, have emergency and school numbers programmed in, but also know an emergency number off by heart in case they lose their phone. If possible, choose a mid-range phone that doesn't make them a target for either thieves or bullies. Your old phone if you upgrade is perfect. If your child needs the accessibility of Apple products, the oldest version still on the market will do everything they need at this stage.

PERSONAL SAFETY

Does your child know your home address and area of the city?

Do they know what to do if they get lost? It might be worth running through some "What if" questions with your child and clarify that they have some idea of what a sensible thing to do would be.

✓ *What if you see a fight on the way home?*

✓ *What if you lose your phone?*

✓ *What if you get lost?*

✓ *What if you miss your stop on the bus?*

✓ *What if you lose your dinner money?*

✓ *What if you can't find your classroom?*

Handout 23

Preparing for food technology in secondary school

You can help improve basic food preparation skills at home and this will stand your child in good stead when he or she starts food technology in secondary school. Time is often tight in these lessons and pupils may not have time to go over basic simple skills that underpin their learning. Think outside the box. There is no correct way of doing things, safety and effectiveness are key. Ask the child or young person (CYP) what works best for them. If you discover a problem area – contact your Habilitation Team who will offer advice and support.

For CYP with even a little useful vision, task lighting and strong contrasts are vital. Wherever possible use a tray to provide contrast, but also to keep everything together for those with little or no vision. Trays are available in a variety of colours, and some even have rubberised bases to reduce sliding. Look for strong contrast and deep sides to prevent spillage.

Remember, these are suggestions, if a child can already successfully complete a task safely, there is no need to change the way they do things.

BREAKFAST

Start with breakfast on days when you don't have to be up and out quickly.

Can your child open a cereal packet and pour cereal into a bowl?

Is he able to open a Tetra Pak® of juice and pour a drink?

Can he use the toaster safely to make toast and spread butter?

Toast is easier to spread than fresh bread. Use spreadable butter. Use a spoon instead of a knife if it is easier.

Don't make it too complicated initially and rehearse the same things until your child gets more confident. But don't make it an ordeal for you both, if you are struggling ask for help.

COOK TOGETHER

Unless you are enthusiastic about real cooking with your child, start off easy with prepacked products like Angel Delight, cookies, or fairy cake packs. Quick and easy, they build confidence both for you and your child, but still develop vital mixing and stirring skills. Take the opportunity to check your child can spoon from one vessel to another. Try a variety of different foodstuffs. Remember deeper spoons hold the contents more easily.

MIXING AND STIRRING

You can use Dycem® as contrast and also to stabilise when mixing or stirring. For some young people holding a bowl steady whilst mixing is difficult. Your Habilitation Team may be able to supply small pieces of Dycem®, otherwise try a damp cloth under the bowl. Durable colourful bowls are available on the high street from Asda to Lakeland and Joseph Joseph®. Choose a bowl that contrasts with the contents being mixed.

CUTTING, CHOPPING, AND SLICING

Although school may have to use colour-coded chopping boards, at home select a board that provides contrast with whatever you are cutting. It makes no sense if you child has some useful vision to chop lettuce on a green board.

Folding chop-and-pot boards are also helpful to move food from the chopping board to the cook pot.

Sharp knives are safer than blunt knives, but if you are concerned, consider specialist learner knives to start with. Look for brands like Kuhn Rikon or KiddiKutter®. Moving on, look for knives that contrast with the board. There are now plenty of knives with brightly coloured blades as well as handles. Remember your child will be using sharp knives and peelers in food technology, so get as much practice in as you can. Ask your Habilitation Team about devices you can use to hold food safely or protect the fingers.

GRATING

Schools tend to use the metal tower graters, but there are many better alternatives for home use that are easier to hold and have a built-in container for whatever you grate. Most major supermarkets offer inexpensive ones like this. If you want to spend more, look for one that comes with a finger guard.

OPENING TINS

Your child will need to practise opening tins, so get him to help you when you are preparing a meal. Use a reliable tin opener like the Culinaire MagiCan that can be used right- or left-handed. Ring pull cans are harder than you might imagine, they need a high degree of force, and the lid can be sharp. They are much more difficult than the smaller ring pulls on canned drinks.

WEIGHING AND MEASURING

Look for large display, talking or balance scales depending on your child's needs. The Cobolt talking scales are not the only options. Look for scales that will allow add and weigh functions, so that all ingredients can be kept together and provide a function for measuring liquid ingredients. Small liquid measurements of more viscous liquids can be done with spoons. Measuring spoons are available in lots of bright colours. Look for ones with a flat base.

POURING HOT AND COLD

There are many different liquid level indicators, (see the Pouring leaflet). Your **Habilitation Specialist** may provide your child with one to use at home when they can use it safely. Make sure your child understands hot and cold and can pour using a jug before progressing. Check your child's skills using cold liquids, before progressing to hot. Encourage safety first, but there are lots of ways to stay safe around hot liquids.

Always assemble everything and use a tray whenever you pour liquids. Use a liquid level indicator – not your finger. Use a mug to learn, rather than a lightweight plastic beaker that will tip. Always practise with cold first.

When pouring from a kettle place the cup or other vessel in the sink and pour from the drainer. Many young people find a water heater an easier option. Look out for Tetley drawstring teabags which are easier and safer to remove.

If your child struggles, a kettle tipper provides safety and confidence to a child learning to pour with boiling water.

Consider purchasing a one-cup water heater at home.

Use a strongly contrasting mug with the handle turning outwards. Try and standardise the mugs used to avoid having to change the slider on the water volume control.

SIMPLE SNACKS

Wraps and sandwiches are a great start. If your child struggles to see butter on the bread, try something like chocolate spread that contrasts well, while he masters spreading. Peeling and slicing fruit is also a good skill to practise. You can combine this with cutting and slicing and make a fruit salad.

USING A MICROWAVE

Introduce the microwave with something like a hot chocolate drink and then move onto mug cakes or mug puddings. Ask the Habilitation Team for help making your microwave accessible to your child. You can also do a range of simple snacks in the microwave like beans on toast or scrambled eggs.

USING THE OVEN

Oven controls should be marked in Tacti-Mark. Bumpons may melt or slide off with grease but can work as a short-term solution.

Allow your child to explore a cold oven before heating it up.

Put protective shelf edges in the oven. These make the shelf edges more visible and reduce injury risks as they don't conduct heat.

Buy long oven gauntlets to protect arms to give extra confidence, but make sure they are not too big for your child to handle dishes safely. As an alternative, look at silicone coated oven gloves. If you child has useful vision look at silicone baking trays. These are lovely and bright and don't conduct heat.

WASHING UP

Most youngsters quite enjoy washing up, but make sure they realise it forms part of the whole task. Make sure they can recognise hot and cold taps and don't fill the sink with hot water. Keep all sharp objects like knives separate in a utensil tub or behind the taps. Never just drop them into the sink.

You can measure a small amount of washing up liquid into the cupped hand or buy one of the scrub-and-dispense brushes. It is possible to feel/hear the dishes squeak when they are clean.

Your Habilitation Specialist can advise on different tasks you can undertake at home to make your child more confident with basic food preparation skills.

Ask for up-to-date recommendations on suitable equipment, utensils and suppliers.

Appendix 3
Let's cook

Let's cook 1

Pouring

Ensure your child is competent pouring cold, before allowing him to move on to hot liquid. Encourage the use of a liquid level indicator, even when pouring cold, to reduce the risk of your child automatically using his fingers when pouring hot. Remember the severity of burns is determined not only by the temperature of the liquid, but also the percentage of the body covered. Younger children burn more easily at lower temperatures and the same amount of liquid affects more of their body. Teach your child what to do if he does burn himself using the "Burns and scalds" handout on pages 147–148.

USING A LIQUID LEVEL INDICATOR

There are several different types of liquid level indicator available from the RNIB shop or Cobolt systems. Some CYPVI prefer one over another. They all work in a similar way, by beeping when the water hits the prongs, and becoming higher pitched or faster as the water rises to the higher contact point. Some make gentle cricket noises and others are quite strident. There is also a range that vibrate too, for students who also have hearing problems. Your **Habilitation Specialist** will be able to advise you on the most suitable device for your child.

Give your child opportunities to explore the liquid level indicator and learn how to place it on the mug or glass. The prongs go into the mug and make contact with the liquid. The battery box always stays on the outside. Beware of lighter plastic beakers that tip easily. If your child has some useful vision look for a mug that contrasts with the tray, and if possible, use a coloured jug too, as with reduced vision water is almost invisible. Demonstrate pouring hand over hand, and make sure the child understands that you pour forwards with a jug, onto the spout and don't turn the hand sideways as you would with a mug going towards the mouth.

Once your child can pour cold reliably, you can progress to hot pouring. You don't need to go straight to a large hot kettle. One-cup water heaters dispense a controlled amount of water and don't require lifting, making them much safer. Very few families now make pots of tea, so there is not the same need for boiling a kettle. See the handout on using the one-cup heater. If you have not got access to one of these, you may like to consider using a travel kettle, which is much lighter, or just adding the necessary amount of water into the kettle.

You may also like to consider using a kettle tipper, which reduces the weight of the kettle and regulates the distance between the kettle and the mug. These are particularly useful if your child has reduced hand strength or cerebral palsy. Your **Habilitation Specialist** or **OT** may have one you can borrow to evaluate at home.

Whatever you are using, allow your child to explore it cold and disconnected from the mains. Learn how to pour accurately from the kettle using cold water first, before heating anything up. You can use Dycem® or Tacti-Mark™ to mark a tray to indicate where the kettle should be and where the mug should be placed.

You may also like to learn hot pouring whilst seated. This reduces the risk of your child wandering away from the workstation with hot liquids.

Using a kettle: Put the kettle on a tray. Add a mug, spoon, liquid level indicator. Have hot chocolate, tea or coffee ready in a designated place. As an alternative to using a tray, you can pour into the sink from the draining board.

Work out beforehand what is the minimum amount of water the kettle needs to boil. It is usually 2 cups, but some now will heat with one large cup of water covering the element.

Start from an empty kettle and add either one or two cups of water into the kettle. Cover all the safety aspects before turning the kettle on. You child should be physically big and strong enough to complete the task successfully. Whilst the kettle is heating, gather any other equipment.

Listen for the noise of the water boiling – you can hear the water bubbling faster and then listen for the click of the kettle turning off. If your child cannot hear these, a gentle hand on the handle will allow them to feel the vibration from the bubbling and the click. Don't pour while the water is still bubbling.

Set the kettle up so your child pours with their stronger hand and keeps the other hand right out of the way. Some young people with useful vision like to hold the mug up to the kettle, so

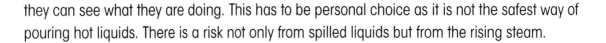

they can see what they are doing. This has to be personal choice as it is not the safest way of pouring hot liquids. There is a risk not only from spilled liquids but from the rising steam.

OTHER TRICKS AND TIPS FOR POURING

As an alternative to a liquid level indicator, if your child has some useful vision, you can put a (clean) table tennis ball in the mug. As the water rises your child may be able to see the ball coming up to the top.

Look for tea bags with strings and tags, to make it easier to remove the teabag from the mug.

When pouring into the sink, use the plug hole to locate the mug and calculate where the kettle needs to be on the drainer to pour into it.

With a teapot or mug, you can put a wooden spoon into the top to provide a way to locate the vessel, and also it will tip out when the water gets to the top.

You can make most hot drinks safely and effectively from cold and heat them up in the microwave to the required temperature. Tea works least well. Make a paste with hot chocolate or coffee, before adding the rest of the water, so it mixes in well.

Let's cook 2

Using the water heater

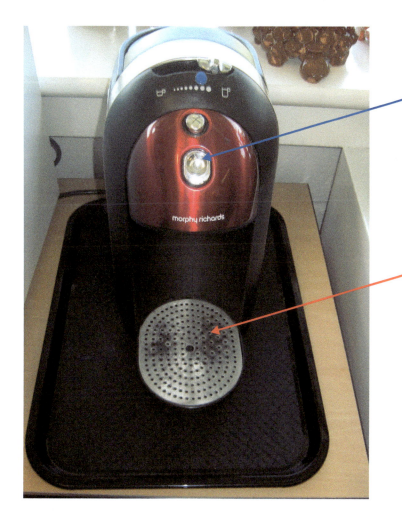

On button

Place cup here

Handle outwards
Do not touch
anything other
than the button
and the cup
handle.

Pre-set the **bumpon** to match the size of the mug. **Do not** slide the lever past the bump-on.

Do not change the cup size. Your cup may overfill.

Make sure there is water in the machine.

Place your prepared cup carefully on the base.

Make sure the handle sticks out to the side.

Press the button.

The light will come on and you will hear the water.

Keep your hands away!

You will hear when it is finished, and the light will go out.

Remove using the cup handle.

Do not use thin plastic vessels, like Pot Noodles, that will get hot and pliable without placing the pot inside a jug.

Boiling water is dangerous. Seek assistance if you are not sure about anything.

Let's cook 3

Tricks and tips

You can help improve basic food preparation skills at home. Think outside the box. There is no correct way of doing things, safety and effectiveness are key. Ask the young person what works best for them. If a child can already successfully complete a task safely, there is no need to change the way they do things.

For children and young people (CYP) with even a little useful vision, task lighting and strong contrasts are vital. Wherever possible, use a tray to provide contrast, as well as to keep everything together for CYP with little or no vision. Trays are available in a variety of colours. Look for contrast and deep sides to prevent spillage. Some trays have rubberised bases that make the tray more secure on the surface. If you have under cupboard lighting, turn it on to provide maximum illumination.

MIXING AND STIRRING

You can use **Dycem**® as contrast and also to stabilise when mixing or stirring. For some young people holding a bowl steady whilst mixing is difficult. If no Dycem® is available to go underneath, try a damp cloth instead. Look for strong colours that will contrast well with ingredients to make the most of residual vision. Joseph Joseph® make some beautiful sets, but they are expensive, so consider supermarket own versions instead.

CHOPPING BOARDS

Chopping boards need to have a designated use, but do not have to follow traditional colour allocation. It is not logical to cut vegetables on a green board and meat on a red one when you need good contrast. Look for non-slip edges and high contrast chopping area. Differentiate between boards with notches or **Tacti-Mark**™ for those with little or no vision.

Folding chop and pot boards are also helpful when transferring from board to dish.

GRATING

Use a grater with a built-in bowl to help keep the food contained. Avoid finger or nail damage by purchasing a grater finger protector.

WEIGHING AND MEASURING

Large display, talking, or balance scales.

The Cobolt traditional talking scales are not the only options. Look for scales that will allow add and weigh functions, so that all ingredients can be kept together. Scales can also provide a function for measuring liquid ingredients like water or milk. Some have a function toggle, but you can simply measure water or milk in grams, as 1 gram (g) is equivalent to 1 millilitre (ml) of water. Milk is slightly heavier, but the difference is so small as to be negligible in recipes. Small measurements of more viscous liquids, like oil can be done with spoons. Salter offers a large display screen on one of their scales at a reasonable price. Measuring spoons are available in lots of bright colours. Look for ones with a flat base.

POURING HOT AND COLD

There are many different liquid level indicators (see the pouring leaflet). Your Habilitation Team may provide your child with one to use at home when they can use it safely. But there are lots of ways to stay safe around hot liquids.

Always start with cold liquids and only move on once a child is confident and safe.

A kettle tipper provides safety and confidence to a blind child learning to pour boiling water from a kettle. These are not cheap, so ask if your Habilitation Team might have one that you could try first. You can progress to a small travel kettle before moving on to free pouring with a kettle. When free pouring from a kettle, place the cup or other vessel in the sink and pour from the drainer. A traditional kettle is not the only alternative.

You may like to consider purchasing a one-cup water heater as many young people find them easier. There are now many varieties on the market.

Use a strongly contrasting mug with the handle turning outwards. Try and standardise the mugs used to avoid having to change the slider on the water volume control and use Tacti-Mark™ or a bumpon to indicate where the slider should be.

Drawstring teabags are easier and safer to remove from a cup. Look for Tetley Easy Squeeze.

USING THE OVEN

Oven controls should be marked in **Tacti-Mark**™. Bumpons may melt or slide off with grease. Allow your child to explore a cold oven before heating it up. Put protective shelf edges in the oven. These make the shelves more visible and offer protection from the hot shelf edge. If your oven has a light, see if it makes it easier for your child to see the shelves.

Buy long oven gauntlets to protect arms and give extra confidence, but make sure they are not so big as to make holding things difficult. Avoid the school type double oven mitts as they are often quite thin and trailing material can be a hazard. You can buy smaller oven gloves specifically made for children.

If your child has useful vision look at silicone baking trays. These are lovely and bright and don't conduct heat. You may find it helpful to place them on top of a standard baking tray when putting them in the oven to reduce wobble.

Before allowing your child to put things in the oven independently, make sure they can carry a loaded baking tray without spilling the contents. It is hard to be sure the tray is level when you can't see. You can set different challenges with items and foodstuffs that move more-or-less easily. You can start off with pompoms or marshmallows and progress to peas or rice to practise keeping contents level.

When opening the oven door, always pull a shelf out a short way to stop the hot door closing on the arm. Always close the door between uses, never leave it open.

WASHING UP

Most youngsters quite enjoy washing up.

Make sure they can recognise hot and cold taps and don't fill the sink with hot water. Start with cold water first. Elastic bands or pipe cleaners work very well to differentiate between taps or use a bumpon on a lever to indicate which way to push.

Keep all sharp objects like knives separate in a utensil tub or behind the taps. Never just drop them into the sink.

You can measure a small amount of washing up liquid into the cupped hand or buy one of the scrub and dispense brushes. You can also transfer washing up liquid into a pump dispenser. It is possible to feel/hear the dishes squeak when they are clean.

Make sure the draining board is clear before your child starts washing up, as it can be difficult to stack dishes safely on top of other items.

Your Habilitation Team can advise on different tasks you can undertake at home to make your child more confident with basic food preparation skills.

Let's cook 4

Cutting, chopping, slicing – the claw grip

EQUIPMENT

Knife with a handle that contrasts with the chopping board

Chopping board contrasting with the food to be cut

USING KNIVES SAFELY

Remember sharp knives are safer than blunt knives which can slip and cause injury. Children and young people should be supervised using knives until they are competent. You can learn the techniques with safety knives first. High contrast is recommended for children and young people with some vision to assist in the process. Make sure your child understands the vocabulary and all the parts of the hand necessary for these techniques. You may need to demonstrate hand over hand or hand under hand to get the correct shape.

THE CLAW GRIP

Practise with something like a banana that presents very little resistance and move on to a cucumber or carrot when more confident. Onions are more difficult because of the curved shape.

Start by shaping your hand as if you are a bear about to claw something. If that doesn't make sense to you, try holding you hand as if you are going to pinch, then bring your other fingers together. Once you have the basic shape, you can start gripping the food you will cut by resting the tips of your fingers on the top and your thumb lower, behind your fingers. Your fingers should be bent, so that the foremost part of your hand is your knuckles, not your fingertips.

Start at one end of the food and gently bring the flat of the knife against your knuckles with the blade pointing down. Slide your claw hand back as the blade slices through the food and prepare for the next slice. You may need to practise getting even slices.

The more you practise, the better you will become.

To see a demonstration of this technique, search in YouTube for "The Claw Grip by British Nutrition:"

https://youtu.be/wVJUD8SSQRA

or "Licence to Cook: Using knife (claw grip):"

https://youtu.be/1PlYOHPTRBQ

Produced by British Nutrition, these videos show foods being safely cut and sliced. They have been developed for encourage primary school children throughout the UK to cook.

Still not confident?

Consider using an onion holder or even a fork to hold the food, keeping fingers away from the blade or purchase a finger shield.

Let's cook 5

Cutting, chopping, slicing – the bridge method

EQUIPMENT

Knife with a handle that contrasts with the chopping board

Chopping board contrasting with the food to be cut

USING KNIVES SAFELY

Remember sharp knives are safer than blunt knives which can slip and cause injury. Children and young people should be supervised using knives until they are competent. Skills can be learned with safety knives before progressing. High contrast is recommended for children and young people with some vision to assist in the process. Make sure your child understands the vocabulary and all the parts of the hand necessary for these techniques. You may need to demonstrate hand over hand or hand under hand to get the correct shape.

THE BRIDGE METHOD

Curl your hand into a caring C. That is the shape you need for a bridge. Create a bridge with the fingers on one side and the thumb on the other. There should be a gap between your hand and the food. Can you get the fingers of your other hand through the gap? Think of it a bit like a train, which will be the knife, going through a tunnel, made by your hand. Make sure the blade of the knife is pointing down towards the food and gently slide it under the bridge. Now slice the food by pressing down and sliding it out of the bridge. This technique works well with rounded food. The first cut is the most difficult, because round things wobble, but after the first cut you will have a flat side, so place that side down on your chopping board and the food will be more stable.

Use this method for tomatoes or apples. You can use it to make the first cut on an onion to cut into half, so that you have a flat slide to place on the board before you swap to the claw technique to slice it up.

Tomatoes cut best with a serrated edge knife. Take the stalk off and turn it over. The top is usually the flattest part.

To see a demonstration of this technique, search in YouTube for "The Bridge hold by British Nutrition," or go to https://youtu.be/uhNvNMOMBg8

Produced by British Nutrition, these videos show foods being safely cut and sliced. They have been developed for encourage primary school children throughout the UK to cook.

Still not confident?

You can use an onion holder, or even a fork to keep your fingers away from the food. You can buy a vegetable slice holder to hold the food and guide your slicing.

Or slice an apple with an apple slicer.

Let's cook 6

Basic food preparation
basic skills sheet 1

Name_____

Tick the skills you can demonstrate

When preparing food:

Fasten hair back ☐

Wash hands ☐

Wipe surfaces ☐

Wear an apron ☐

Use a recipe ☐

Handle equipment safely ☐

Assemble all equipment and ingredients ☐

Wash up ☐

Let's cook 7

My skills sheet 2

Name_____

Tick the skills you can complete safely:

Spread with a spoon ☐

Spread with a knife ☐

Slice or chop using ☐

Onion holder ☐

Bridge technique ☐

Claw technique ☐

Grate ☐

Use a peeler ☐

Use a tin opener

Use measuring spoons

Use measuring cups

Weigh

Mix

Whisk

Use a microwave

Use a toaster

Use a one-cup water heater

Use the oven

Let's cook 8

My skills sheet 3

Name_____

Tick the devices you can use safely

Small electrical devices:

Use a blender

Use a mixer

Use a toastie maker

Use a kettle

Use a kitchen timer

Use a steamer

Use a slow cooker

Use a George Foreman grill

Use a single-induction hob

Using the cooker:

Use the oven

Use the hob

Use the grill

Store food correctly:

In the cupboard

In the fridge

In the freezer

Let's cook 9

Hot drink in the microwave – hot chocolate or coffee

EQUIPMENT	INGREDIENTS
Microwave	2 spoons of hot chocolate
Cup/mug or spoon	1 spoon of coffee
Tray	Milk
Liquid level indicator	Sugar (to taste)
(Optional)	Water

Gather all equipment and ingredients onto a tray.

Add two spoons of chocolate or one spoon of coffee into the cup. Check the instructions on the pack as brands vary, and choose an appropriately sized spoon.

Add a small amount of milk and mix to a paste. Add sugar to taste.

Use a liquid level indicator if you need it.

Microwave for one minute*.

Allow to stand for one minute before drinking. Cream, marshmallows, and sprinkles are optional!

*The length of time needed depends on your microwave power. Start with one minute and add extra time if necessary.

Skills: spooning from one vessel to another, mixing, using the microwave

Let's cook 10

Tuna and sweetcorn wrap

INGREDIENTS	EQUIPMENT
1 small tin of tuna	A mixing bowl
2 tablespoons of tinned sweetcorn	A tablespoon
1 tablespoon of mayonnaise	A plate
Tortilla wrap(s)	
Optional seasoning – salt, pepper	

Drain any liquid off the tuna. You can do this with a can strainer or drainer lid or by pouring it carefully into a colander over the sink. Measure, then spoon the mayonnaise and sweetcorn into the bowl. Mix the tuna, sweetcorn, and mayonnaise together in the bowl. Taste the mix to see if the ratio is right and add salt and pepper if desired. You can add extra mayonnaise or sweetcorn if you prefer.

Put your wrap on the plate. If your wrap is a bit stiff, microwave it for 10 seconds so it rolls more easily. Spread the wrap with a little bit more mayonnaise. This will act like glue to hold the wrap together. Spread your tuna filling into the middle of the wrap and roll the wrap round the filling. You can eat it whole or cut into sections if you prefer.

Skills: opening tins, draining, measuring, mixing and spreading, using the microwave.

Let's cook 11

Easy-cook pizza for one

INGREDIENTS	EQUIPMENT
Naan or pitta bread	Small convection/fan oven or microwave
Tomato puree	Grater
50 g cheese	Knife
Choice of toppings	Spoon
	Pizza or baking tray
	Chopping board
	Optional – tin opener and onion holder

METHOD

Prepare your toppings first. These will need chopping or slicing. Suggested toppings could include onions, peppers, mushrooms, ham, pineapple, sweetcorn. You can use an onion holder to slice the ingredients if you wish.

You may prefer to use tinned pineapple or sweetcorn, in which case you will need a tin opener. You may choose to slice, rip, or cut ham with scissors.

Put the oven on at 200°C/gas mark 6 to heat.

Grate your cheese. You may like to use a bigger piece of cheese to make it easier to hold or you can use a grater safety holder.

Systematically spread the tomato puree or pizza topping on the naan or pitta. You can go from the centre and spread outwards, or from the edges round and inwards. The puree contrasts well with the base so you may be able to see if the base is covered; if not, feel gently with your fingertips to ensure it is all covered.

Spread your toppings evenly across the base. Sprinkle the cheese on top.

Put your pizza on a pizza dish or baking tray and cook in the oven for 10 minutes. Set a timer to tell you when it's ready.

If you want to want to microwave your pizza, place it on a microwaveable plate and cook for 1 or 2 minutes depending on the size of your pizza.

Tick the off skills you have used on your "Let's cook skill sheet."

Skills: chopping, slicing, opening tins, grating, using an oven or a microwave safely, using a timer.

Let's cook 12

Microwave scrambled eggs for one

INGREDIENTS	EQUIPMENT
1 extra large egg or 2 small eggs	Microwave oven
1 tsp milk	Microwave pan, jug, or mixing bowl
Pinch of salt	Whisk or fork
Pinch of black pepper	Spatula or fork
½ tsp butter (optional)	

METHOD

Break egg(s) into microwave pan, jug, or mixing bowl. Hold the egg in your hand over the bowl and give the egg a confident tap, press your thumbs into the crack and separate the egg from the shell. If you work over the bowl the egg should slide in gently as you pull it apart. Add milk, salt, and pepper. Beat well with whisk or fork. Add butter to mixture if desired.

Cook for 30 seconds at 100% power, stir with the spatula, and cook again for 30 seconds at 100% power. Mix egg well with a rubber spatula and serve. The egg will be moist. If dry eggs are preferred, cook 5 seconds more at 100% power. Mix with rubber spatula and serve.

Timings are approximate depending on the power of your microwave.

Serve on toast. Add grated cheese or shredded smoked salmon as a variation

Skills: breaking an egg, mixing, whisking, using the microwave.

Let's cook 13

Chocolate mug cake

INGREDIENTS	EQUIPMENT
45 g self-raising flour (3 tbsp)	A microwaveable mug
30 g caster sugar (2 tbsp)	A spoon
15 g cocoa powder (1 tbsp)	A microwave
1 tbsp sunflower oil (15 ml)	
4 tbsp whole milk * (45 ml)	
Chunks of chocolate	

INSTRUCTIONS

1. In a mug, add all the ingredients, apart from the chunks of chocolate and mix them all together

2. Add a few chunks of chocolate into the middle. It's lovely with two pieces of white, and two pieces of milk chocolate

3. Microwave for 60–90 seconds. And enjoy!

Serve with ice cream or squirty cream.

*you can use non-dairy alternatives if you prefer.

Skills: weighing and measuring, mixing, and using the microwave.

Let's cook 14

Microwave baked potato with optional cheese and beans

INGREDIENTS

One large potato

Butter for serving

Optional grated cheese and baked beans – microwave pot

METHOD

Wash and thoroughly dry the potato. Stab the potato with a fork three or four times (this lets the steam escape and stops it exploding in the microwave).

Microwave on high power for 4 minutes, then turn it over and microwave for another 3 minutes. The potato should give (be slightly soft) to the touch. If not, cook it again for one minute and repeat until cooked. You can set a timer on Alexa or your phone if you prefer. Let it stand for a minute.

Always use an oven glove to remove the potato from the microwave. It will be very hot.

If you want cheese and beans, grate your cheese beforehand (or use pre-grated cheese) and cook your microwave beans on high power for one minute. While the potato is standing. It will stay hot. The bean pot will get very hot, so use a glove to remove from the microwave and open it carefully. Slice your potato and add your butter, cheese, and beans to taste.

As an alternative, you can microwave your potato for 3 minutes each side, then cook it in the oven for 30 minutes on 200°C (gas mark 6) which will give you a crispy skin.

Let's cook 15

Flapjack

INGREDIENTS	EQUIPMENT
110 g butter	Bowl
40 g sugar	Wooden mixing spoon
2 tablespoons (30 ml) golden syrup	Scales
175 g rolled oats/porridge oats	Measuring spoon
Optional – raisins, chocolate chips	Shallow baking tin/tray greaseproof paper

Cut a piece of greaseproof paper, just bigger than the size of baking tin – scissors may be easier than using the cutter built into the packaging. A 20 cm square tin is ideal for this recipe. Line the tin with the paper. Turn the oven on to 180°C or gas mark 4.

Using a microwaveable bowl on the scales to weigh your ingredients, add the butter, sugar, and syrup. Microwave the mixture for 30 seconds and stir to check if the butter has melted – it will gradually become easier to stir if it has melted. If not, microwave another 10 seconds, stir, and repeat until melted. Mix thoroughly and return to the scales to add the remaining ingredients.

Stir well until it becomes a thick and sticky mixture. Pour or spoon the mixture into the baking tray and flatten it down with the back of your spoon. Try and get an even height and reach right to the corners.

Place the flapjack in the oven and cook for 15 minutes, or until golden brown. Allow to cool before lifting out of the tray and cutting into slices.

Skills: weighing and measuring, mixing, spooning from one vessel to another, using the oven.

Let's cook 16

Cheese and ham toasties

Toastie maker

Bread

Ham

Cheese

Butter

METHOD

Put the toastie maker on, with the plates down, a light will come on to show it is heating. A second light will come on when it is hot and it may click.

If you can't see the lights, get someone to help you time how long the toastie maker takes to warm up. Note it down and then set a timer on Alexa or your phone.

While waiting for it to heat up, butter two pieces of bread – butter side out. Add filling of cheese and ham to the inside.

When it's hot, carefully lift the sandwich onto the hot plates.

Close the plates and cook the toastie for 4 minutes. Use Alexa or your phone as a timer.

Lift the toastie out carefully using large silicone tongs or a large slice.

The cheese will be **very** hot, so wait a minute before eating.

Skills: spreading, safe use of small electrical cooking device, using a timer.

Glossary

WHO/WHAT/WHERE	DESCRIPTION
7–38–55 Rule	Albert Mehrabian *Silent Messages: Implicit Communication of Emotions and Attitudes*. Wadsworth. Jul 1972. From a brief summary see Mulder, P. (2012). *7 38 55 Rule of Communication*. Retrieved [16.04.21] from toolshero: www.toolshero.com/communication-skills/7-38-55-rule/ Mehrabian asserted 7% of what we communicate consists of the literal content of the message. The use of one's voice, such as tone, intonation, and volume, take up 38% and as much as 55% of communication consists of body language.
Attention difficulties/ ADHD	Attention Deficit Hyperactivity Disorder (ADHD) is a behavioural disorder that includes symptoms such as inattentiveness, hyperactivity, and impulsiveness. Symptoms of ADHD tend to be noticed at an early age and may become more noticeable when a child's circumstances change, such as when they start school.
Autistic Spectrum Condition (ASC)	Also referred to as Autistic Spectrum Disorder (ASD). Some children with severe sight impairment show traits of ASC, but do not have a diagnosis, because it stems from lack of knowledge of the world and improves over time. Some children may have sight impairment and an ASC diagnosis.
Backward chaining	See **Chaining**.
British Association of Teachers of the Deaf (BATOD)	BATOD is the only association in the United Kingdom that represents the interests of teachers of deaf children and young people:www.batod.org.uk/information/training-as-a-teacher-of-the-deaf/
Braille	Braille is a tactile reading and writing system, created by Louis Braille in the 19th century and still in use today. It can be produced on a Perkins Brailler or on an electronic device like a BrailleNote. It works by producing a series of raised dots using variations of a six-dot cell.
British Blind Sport (BBS)	Go to britishblindsport.org.uk/ for information on early movement programmes, including First Steps and Jangles.
CAMHS (Child and Adolescent Mental Health Service)	CAMHS is likely to be involved if your child has an ASC (Autism Spectrum Condition) diagnosis or has other acute mental health issues.

WHO/WHAT/WHERE	DESCRIPTION
Cerebra	Cerebra is the national charity helping children with brain conditions and their families discover a better life together. It provides plenty of good advice on its website and is particularly good on sleep issues. It offers a specialist one-to-one advice and support service for children with certain diagnoses (https://cerebra.org.uk/get-advice-support/sleep-advice-service/, cerebra.org.uk/).
CFVI **Curriculum Framework** **for CYP with VI**	Published on 15 March 2022, there is only a passing reference in this book to the Curriculum Framework for Children and Young People with Vision Impairment. The Curriculum Framework for Children and Young People with Vision Impairment (CFVI) has been developed to support children and young people with vision impairment access an appropriate and equitable education. The project was launched by the RNIB in 2020 in conjunction with VIEW, Victar, and Thomas Pocklington, establishing a single UK-wide Curriculum Framework for CYPVI. The framework presents outcomes within 11 teaching areas: Facilitating an Inclusive World Sensory Development Communication Literacy Habilitation: Orientation and Mobility Habilitation: Independent Living Skills Accessing Information Technology Health: Social, Emotional, Mental, and Wellbeing Social, Sports, and Leisure Preparing for Adulthood It provides a shared vocabulary to be used by children and young people, their families and professionals in the UK who work with them. A shared vocabulary supports both better communication and purpose. At the heart of the framework is a set of three fundamental aims: To help clarify and define the elements of specialist skill development, interventions and best practice support that are considered to be essential for children and young people with vision impairment To assist qualified specialist practitioners in raising the awareness amongst other professionals and parents of the need for children and young people with vision impairment to be taught skills that enable them to access the curriculum and the wider world with as much independence as possible To aid discussions and understanding amongst all involved in a child/young person's education of how and when these skills should be taught by suitably qualified specialists and reinforced by non-specialists.

WHO/WHAT/WHERE	DESCRIPTION
Chaining	When teaching any complex task, it is necessary to break it into small component parts. These tasks are taught separately but are sequential. Teaching them step by step is known as chaining. Success is key to progress, so you start with the element the child is most likely to achieve. Forward chaining starts with the beginning of the task sequence. After each step is mastered, instruction begins at the next step. The remainder of the task is completed each time by the adult modelling and explaining actions. Backward chaining starts with learning the final component and working backwards through the components. Jerry Webster, "Chaining Forward and Chaining Backwards." *ThoughtCo*, 30 January 2019. www.thoughtco.com/chaining-forward-and-chaining-backwards-3110581
Changing Places	To use the toilet in safety and comfort, some people need to be able to access Changing Places, which have more space and the right equipment, including a height-adjustable changing bench and a hoist. You can find more information and locations on www.changing-places.org/
Child protection	See **Safeguarding**.
Childline	Childline, the child-facing support service of the NSPCC offers free, confidential advice and support to children and young people under 18, whenever or whatever they need help with **0800 1111**.
Code of Practice (SEND)	Department for Education/Department of Health (2015) *Special Educational Needs and Disability Code of Practice: 0 to 25 Years*, January. London: DfE/DoH. https://assets.publishing.service.gov.uk/government/uploads/system/uploads/attachment_data/file/398815/SEND_Code_of_Practice_January_2015.pdf **This Code of Practice provides statutory guidance on duties, policies and procedures relating to Part 3 of the Children and Families Act 2014 and associated regulations and applies to England. It relates to children and young people with special educational needs (SEN) and disabled children and young people. It provides the framework for EHC Plans**. **It is currently under review**.
CYPVI	Abbreviation for **Children and Young People with Vision Impairment**

WHO/WHAT/WHERE	DESCRIPTION
Dexterity	Manual dexterity is the ability to make small, precise, coordinated hand and finger movements to grasp and manipulate objects. Development of these skills occurs over time, primarily during childhood. It requires motor planning and complex execution of a task.
Dycem®	Provides a grip to keep dishes and devices stable on a surface and can provide a strong contrast. Dycem® material is used to help stabilise objects, hold objects firmly in place, or to provide a better grip. Available from: https://shop.rnib.org.uk/ or www.nrshealthcare.co.uk
Education Health and Care Plan (EHCP)	The Education Health Care Plan replaced the Statement of Special Educational Needs. It is a legal document in England that describes a child or young person's special educational, health, and social care needs and shows how those needs will be met. They can apply to children and young people between the ages of 0 and 25.
England	See Code of Practice, EHCP, and school years in England.
Emotional literacy	Emotional literacy is the term used to describe the ability to understand and express feelings. It requires children to recognise their own feelings and manage them and is a skill that all children need to develop. There are five main aspects of emotional intelligence which, when developed, lead to children becoming emotionally literate. In his book *Emotional Intelligence*, Daniel Goleman identifies: • Knowing emotions – a child recognises a feeling as it happens • Managing emotions – a child has ways of reassuring themselves when they feel anxious or upset • Self-motivation – a child is in charge of their emotions, rather than controlled by them • Empathy – a child is aware of what another person is feeling • Handling relationships – child is able to build relationships with others See also: www.elsa-support.co.uk/www.parentkind.org.uk/blog/8719/Helping-children-develop-emotional-literacy
Guide Dogs: Children and Young People's Services	Guide Dogs Children and Young People's Services provides habilitation and other support to CYPVI, either independently or through local authority contracts. Guide dogs and buddy dogs are available to qualifying children and young people. www.guidedogs.org.uk/getting-support/
Habilitation Assistant	A Habilitation Assistant provides work to children and families under the direction of the Habilitation Specialist.

WHO/WHAT/WHERE	DESCRIPTION
Habilitation Specialist	A Habilitation Specialist holds a professional qualification and should be registered as a Qualified Habilitation Specialist, RQHS with HabilitationVIUK. They teach orientation and mobility skills and independent living skills at home and at school, depending on where you child is educated. This can include teaching a child how to use a cane, teaching specific routes around school, or the local area, road safety, personal safety, and the range of life skills in this book. The Habilitation Specialist may be employed by the Local Authority, by a registered Charity, like Guide Dogs, or could be freelance.
Habilitation VIUK	This is the professional body for UK Habilitation Specialists and assistants. It represents the needs of its members, promotes awareness of habilitation and maintains standards. There are webpages for parents and professionals. www.habilitationviuk.org.uk
Hand over hand	When you use the hand-over-hand technique to help your child do an activity, you place your hands over your child's hands. Wherever possible, work from behind your child. Your child is the one who is touching the materials, and your hands guide them as they manipulate the materials to complete the activity. As you find they are able to do small parts of the activity, you can lessen the support your hands provide by pulling your hands away or moving them to their wrist or arm. In that way, your hands are ready to come back and lend support if your child needs assistance.
Hand under hand	When you use the hand-under-hand technique, your hands perform the activity while your child's hands rest on top of yours – this way, your child can feel what your hands are doing. If the activity is new to your child and they are hesitant to try it, they may feel more secure touching your hands rather than the unknown object or activity. Also, because their palms are on your hands, they'll be able to focus their energy on feeling the movements of your hands. They may also feel more comfortable and in control because they can freely remove their hands if they want to. As you perform the activity, describe what you are doing with your hands. Always try to work from behind your child, or alongside, if possible.
Incidental Learning	Incidental Learning is what a child absorbs from watching and mimicking parents, siblings, or peers. The vast majority of learning usually comes through vision, but this information stream is lost to children with severe vision impairment. These children need to be specifically taught many elements that other children just assimilate. It can mean that children and young people develop at a slower rate and have less understanding of the world around them, without targeted intervention.

WHO/WHAT/WHERE	DESCRIPTION
IPSEA (Independent Provider of Special Education Advice)	IPSEA offers independent legally based advice, support, and training to help get the right education for children and young people with special educational needs. It offers a unique range of services developed to make sure that families, and those advising them, understand children and young people's legal rights and entitlements to education provision.www.ipsea.org.uk/
Learned Helplessness	Learned helplessness occurs when an individual continuously faces a negative, uncontrollable situation and stops trying to change their circumstances, even when they have the ability to do so. The term was coined in 1967 by the American psychologists Martin Seligman and Steven Maier. The pair were conducting research on animal behaviour that involved delivering electric shocks to dogs. Dogs who learned that they couldn't escape the shock stopped trying in subsequent experiments, even when it became possible to avoid the shock by jumping over a barrier. In this context it can stem from wrapping a child in cotton wool, not allowing them to try to undertake tasks independently or intervening before they can achieve it successfully. www.psychologytoday.com/gb/basics/learned-helplessness
Local Offer	Every Local Authority (LA) has a statutory obligation to have and promote the Local Offer on its website. It should bring together information in one place about health, education and social care for: children and young people from birth to 25 years old who have a Special Educational Need or Disability (SEND) parents and carers of children with SEND. It should include information on support services, and how to access them, as well as details on special or specialist schools and resource bases.
Look UK	Look supports young visually impaired people and their families to thrive. They do this through mentoring, transformational events, youth forums and parent support groups. www.look-uk.org/
National Quality Standards for Habilitation Training (2011 and 2022)	These Quality Standards are designed to make sure that children and young people with visual impairment are enabled (through high-quality mobility and independence training and support) to achieve the greatest possible independence and maximise their education https://habilitationviuk.org.uk/wp-content/uploads/2022/05/Habilitation-Quality-Standards-2nd-edition.pdfal outcomes and life chances. The Standards were updated in May 2022 and can be found here https://habilitationviuk.org.uk/wp-content/uploads/2022/05/Habilitation-Quality-Standards-2nd-edition.pdf

WHO/WHAT/WHERE	DESCRIPTION
NSPCC (National Society for the Prevention of Cruelty to Children)	PANTS is an acronym that helps children understand that their body belongs to them, and they should tell someone they trust if anything makes them feel upset or worried. PANTS https://learning.nspcc.org.uk/research-resources/schools/pants-teaching PANTS (the Underwear Rule) lesson plan, slide presentation, curriculum links, classroom activities, and supporting information. It's Not OK https://learning.nspcc.org.uk/research-resources/schools/its-not-ok Teaching resources about positive relationships, how to recognise concerning or abusive behaviour and what to do about it for use with children and young people aged 11+. Love Life https://learning.nspcc.org.uk/research-resources/schools/love-life Films and activities to help young people with special educational needs and learning disabilities learn about emotions, relationships, and identity. If you're worried about a child, even if you're unsure, contact NSPCC professional counsellors for help, advice, and support. Call **0808 800 5000** or email help@nspcc.org.uk. Childline offers free, confidential advice and support to children and young people under 18, whenever or whatever they need help with.**0800 1111**.
Objects of reference	These are tactile objects that reinforce understanding of activities, things, or locations. Your child may have a tactile timetable in school. Some suggestions for objects of reference: • Swimsuit for swimming • Pumps/trainers for PE • Toilet roll for toilet • Flannel for bath or washing Try and avoid transient objects of reference that may build in limits or cause confusion. For instance, don't use a nappy for the toilet and don't use armbands for swimming (because they become redundant: a child gets potty-trained and learns to swim).
Occupational therapist (OT)	Occupational therapists treat injured, ill, or disabled CYP through the therapeutic use of everyday activities. They help them develop, recover, improve (as well as maintain) the skills needed for daily living and working. In some cases, they can advise on adaptations in the home to make daily living tasks easier.
Paediatrician	A consultant doctor who specialises in the care of children and young people.
Paths to Literacy	Free strategies and resources to help your child learn. www.pathstoliteracy.org/

WHO/WHAT/WHERE	DESCRIPTION
Perkins Brailler	The Perkins School for the Blind is the home of the Perkins Brailler. It is primarily a day and residential school (in Massachusetts) for children and young people with vision impairment. They also offer helpful blogs, a wide range of resources, and links to other useful sites, as well as their educational hub (which includes Paths to Literacy, which holds a phenomenal range of resources and ideas).www.perkins.org/
PfA Preparation for Adulthood	Funded by the Department for Education (DfE), PfA provides expertise and support to local authorities and their partners to embed preparing for adulthood from the earliest years. They work to ensure that young people with SEND achieve paid employment, independent living, housing options, good health, friendships, relationships, and community inclusion. www.preparingforadulthood.org.uk/
Pica	Pica is an eating disorder in which a person chews or eats things not usually considered food. It is often associated with autism. It is not unusual for small children to put non-food items (like grass or toys) in their mouths to explore them, because they're curious about the world around them and get better feedback orally. This is a normal developmental phase. Children and young people with pica continue beyond that phase and can sometimes eat things that can lead to health problems.
PRK	Prior relevant knowledge.
Physiotherapist	A physiotherapist helps restore movement and function when someone is affected by injury, illness, or disability. You can access physiotherapy through your GP, by self-referral, or via a specialist (depending on how your local NHS systems are set up). Some special schools have specialist physiotherapists based on site. You can also obtain physiotherapy privately.
Proprioception	Proprioception uses the feedback from muscles and joints and works in conjunction with the vestibular system to enable the brain to calculate the body's position in relation to balance, direction, movement, and force. In simple terms: • It allows the brain to work out how much force it needs to grasp and pick up a raw eggshell without breaking it • It enables the calculations that adjust leg extension and stride to run up a hill without falling

WHO/WHAT/WHERE	DESCRIPTION
Protective Behaviours	Protective Behaviours is a safety awareness and resilience-building programme. It helps children and adults to recognise any situation where they feel worried or unsafe, such as feeling stressed, bullied, or threatened, and explores practical ways to keep safe. Children are taught that they can talk about anything, no matter how big or small, to their chosen safe people. It encourages the use of correct medical terminology from an early age for genitals and other body parts, to avoid confusion.www.protectivebehaviours.org/what-does-protective-behaviours-mean
QTVI (Qualified Teacher of Vision Impaired) or **TOVI teacher of vision impaired**	QTVI is a mandatory qualification for those exclusively teaching children and young people with vision impairments. All children with SVI should have access to a QTVI from time to time. Find out more about the role from the RNIB:www.rnib.org.uk/services-we-offer-advice-professionals/education-professionals
RADAR Key	Many disabled toilets are locked with a RADAR key to ensure they are available for disabled people when necessary, and to prevent damage. There is more room, and they are quite often cleaner than other public toilets. These keys are universal – you may be able to obtain one through Social Care, from Disability Rights UK, the Blue Badge Company or on Amazon, but always ensure they are genuine RADAR keys. If your child is bigger or needs more support, look into Changing Places (see above).
Resource base (VI base within a school)	A number of mainstream schools contain resource bases within them. The student attends a mainstream school but is afforded additional support through the resource base. In the case of VI bases, there should be a QTVI (see above) on site and support varies depending on need but can include facilitating a student to access what is on the board or teaching Braille or touch typing.
RNIB (Royal National Institute of Blind People)	The RNIB offers a variety of support services and leaflets and campaigns on behalf of those with vision impairment. The RNIB has pages for people with sight loss, and their families and professionals:www.rnib.org.uk/
RNID	After a brief name change to Action on Hearing Loss, the RNID reverted back to its official title, the Royal National Institute for Deaf People. It is a charitable organisation working on behalf of the UK's 9 million people who are deaf, have hearing loss, or tinnitus.

WHO/WHAT/WHERE	DESCRIPTION
Safeguarding	All schools or other organisations working with children must undertake regular safeguarding training and be cognisant of the relevant statutory guidance. In schools it is the *Keeping Children Safe in Education* document, which is revised annually: www.gov.uk/government/publications/keeping-children-safe-in -education--2Staff should all hold enhanced DBS (Disclosure and Barring Service) status. A full list of government current safeguarding documents can be found at: www.gov.uk/topic/ schools-colleges-childrens-services/safeguarding-children In Scotland children are safeguarded under GIRFEC (Getting it Right for Every Child) see **Scotland** below
Safety	For advice on keeping your child safe: • Child Accident Prevention Trust: www.capt.org.uk/ • Dog, Duck & Cat Trust: www.dogduckandcat.co.uk/ • Family Lives: www.familylives.org.uk/advice/primary/health -and-development/keeping-your-child-safe/ • NSPCC: www.nspcc.org.uk/keeping-children-safe/ • NSPCC PANTS rule: www.nspcc.org.uk/keeping-children-safe/ support-for-parents/underwear-rule/ • Protective Behaviours: www.protectivebehaviours.org/ • Thinkuknow online safety: www.thinkuknow.co.uk/4_7/
Scaffolding	In education, scaffolding refers to a variety of instructional techniques used to move students progressively toward stronger understanding, and ultimately greater independence, in the learning process. The term itself offers the relevant descriptive metaphor: Teachers or other supporters provide successive levels of temporary support that help students reach higher levels of comprehension and skill acquisition that they would not be able to achieve without assistance. Like physical scaffolding, the supportive strategies are incrementally removed when they are no longer needed, and the teacher gradually shifts more responsibility over the learning process to the student.
School nurse	Parents and schools in the UK have access to a school nurse team. They take over from the health visiting team as the child moves to school, offering advice and support on a range of topics – such as like sleep problems, constipation, and toileting – as well as delivering the school vaccination programmes.

WHO/WHAT/WHERE	DESCRIPTION
School years in England	School years in England run from 1 September each year. The statutory school age is 5–16 (pupils are strongly encouraged to stay in education to 18). Most children start school at age 4 and are deemed to be "rising 5s." Infants and Juniors are primary school pupils. Secondary begins at Year 7 in most authorities. Prior to statutory school age, children may attend preschool, nursery, or *Foundation Stage* between ages 2 and 4. *Infants – Key Stage 1* (Reception pupils will be 5 during the academic year; Year 1 pupils will be 6; Year 2 pupils will be 7). *Juniors – Key Stage 2* (Year 3 pupils will be 8 during the academic year; Year 4 pupils will be 9; Year 5 pupils will be 10; Year 6 pupils will be 11). See the School years grid at the end of the Glossary to compare school years in other nations
Scotland	**An Individualised Educational Programme** (or **IEP**) is used by many schools in Scotland as a planning and monitoring tool for children with additional support needs. A **Coordinated Support Plan** (or **CSP**) is an education plan prepared by local authorities for certain **children** and young people with additional support needs. The plan outlines their additional support needs, objectives that have been set for them to achieve. Getting it right for every child (**GIRFEC**) supports families by making sure children and young people can receive the right help, at the right time, from the right people. The aim is to help them to grow up feeling loved, safe and respected, so that they can realise their full potential. www.gov.scot/policies/girfec/Wellbeing (SHANARRI) The GIRFEC approach supports children and young people so that they can grow up feeling loved, safe, and respected and can realise their full potential. At home, in school, or the wider community, every child and young person should be: Safe Healthy Achieving Nurtured Active Respected Responsible Included These eight factors are often referred to by their initial letters – SHANARRI. Scottish school years run from August to June. See also VINCYP

WHO/WHAT/WHERE	DESCRIPTION
SENCo **Special Educational Needs Coordinator**	A Special Educational Needs Coordinator (SENCo) is an experienced qualified teacher who is responsible for special educational needs provision in school. Every school in the UK is obliged to employ a SENCO as they ensure all students with learning disabilities are well equipped to obtain the right help and support they need at school. Also sometimes known as a SENDCo, both have had additional training in special needs and disabilities.
SENDIASS **Special Educational Needs and Disabilities Information Advice and Support Services**	SENDIASS offer information, advice, and support for parents and carers of children and young people with special educational needs and disabilities (SEND). This service is also offered directly to young people. The service is free, impartial and confidential. KIDS SENDIASS have developed resources providing information and advice for parents, carers, professionals, and young people. It is a legal requirement that all local authorities have a SENDIASS service and KIDS provides a number of these services across the country. Each KIDS SENDIASS service has a local page with its contact details, local information, and local resources. www.kids.org.uk/sendiass
Sense	Sense provides support and information as well as activities and respite for everyone living with complex disabilities or who is deafblind. It offers support and activities for CYP with MSI and their families.www.sense.org.uk/
Sensory avoidance	Some children are oral avoidant or defensive. They may hate certain textures and have trouble with solid food. Some children do not like to be touched, and others will avoid touching certain textures. This used to be called tactile defensiveness, but it is recognised as a much wider issue now and is termed sensory avoidance. Some children hate loud noise or become overwhelmed if there are too many different noises. Ear defenders may help, but children with sight impairment need to use their hearing as much as possible. Other children will not go into a bathroom that has a hand dryer. You may find the school has to turn them off (because your child cannot predict when they will come on). The child may need a sensory assessment from an occupational therapist (see above), who may recommend a sensory diet (see below).
Sensory diet	A range of activities planned by a specialist occupational therapist (see above) to help a child with sensory issues feel more comfortable, or be alert or calm, at the correct times. It can form part of a sensory integration programme.

WHO/WHAT/WHERE	DESCRIPTION
Sensory seeking	Some children enjoy and seek out particular sensations. Oral sensory seekers will put everything in their mouths. Some children love the sound and vibration from a hand dryer or hair dryer. Occasionally they may forget to return from the bathroom, because they have become fascinated by the noise of the dryer. Other children need physical pressure or weight to be comfortable. They may like to squeeze up close or request hugs. The child may need a sensory assessment from an occupational therapist (see above), who may recommend a sensory diet (see above).
Sensory integration	Jean Ayres defined sensory integration as "The neurological process that organises sensation from one's own body and from the environment and makes it possible to use the body effectively with the environment." Effectively, this means that the brain organises all the different sensory inputs to make sense of everything and enables the body to do what it needs to do. There are many more senses than most people realise. However, usually vision is the one that ties all the inputs together, so children with severe vision impairments may be at a significant disadvantage when integrating the senses. www.sensoryintegrationeducation.com/
Severe sight impairment (SSI)	The term used on the formal Certificate of Vision Impairment (CVI) registration document as an alternative to 'blind'. 'Blind' implies no vision at all, which is only rarely the case. Occasionally seen as SVI – severe vision impairment
Sight impaired	This replaces "partially sighted" on the registration document (see severe sight impairment above).
Sleep	Children aged between 6 and 13 need between 9 and 11 hours of sleep a night. Sleep can be a problem for many children, but particularly those with certain conditions or a poor understanding of time. Children with no perception of light often struggle to differentiate between day and night. The following organisations all provide support. sleepcouncil.org.uk/ sleepcouncil.org.uk/sleep-advice-scenarios/meet-daisy-sleep-advice-for-children/ Cerebra also provides specialist advice and support on sleep: cerebra.org.uk/download/sleep-a-guide-for-parents/ Your GP, paediatrician, or school nurse (see entries above) will also be able to advise on sleep.
SOS!SEN	SOS!SEN offers a free, friendly, independent and confidential telephone helpline for parents and others looking for information and advice on Special Educational Needs and Disability (SEND). sossen.org.uk/

WHO/WHAT/WHERE	DESCRIPTION
Special school	Special schools offer specialist provision to meet particular needs. They have small classes and specialist staff.www.goodschoolsguide.co.uk/special-educational-needs/schools/special-schools
Speech and language therapist (SaLT)	Speech and language therapists provide life-changing treatment, support, and care for children and adults who have difficulties with communication, or with eating, drinking and swallowing.
Tactile learner	Tactile learners learn primarily through touch or verbal input and have no access to print and very limited visual images. They will probably use Braille or need access to speech on computers.
Tacti-Mark™	Durable tactile marking up liquid. Sets to hard. Available from RNIB in orange or black
Transition	Transition is the process of moving from one state or setting to another – for instance, moving from home to school, or from primary to secondary school. It is a time of change that can have a great deal of impact on a child.
Vestibular system	The vestibular system is one of the body's senses. It is located in the inner ear and is the main contributor to the sense of balance and spatial orientation. It tells the body where it is in space and which way up it is, in order to coordinate movement and balance. The brain uses information from the vestibular system (along with proprioception) to calculate exact force and movement. Vestibular system dysfunction can cause vertigo and motion sickness.
VICTA Parent Portal	This is a one-stop information hub for all parents and carers raising a child who is blind or partially sighted. It has a wealth of information covering topics from early years to assistive technology and directs readers to many other organisations which can help.www.victa.org.uk/introducing-victa-parent-portal/
VICTAR	Vision Impairment Centre for Teaching and Research, University of Birmingham VICTAR has a long record of leading innovative and influential UK and international research. Significant and recent funded research projects include longitudinal work with young people as they leave compulsory education; national surveys and employment; development of early child development and teaching services in countries of the global south; development of reading assessments; and international literature reviews. It was also instrumental in the creation of the **CFVI**. www.birmingham.ac.uk/research/victar/index.aspx

WHO/WHAT/WHERE	DESCRIPTION
VINCYP	Based in Scotland, VINCYP aims to improve the care for children and young people with a visual impairment. VINCYP involves professionals working in health, education and social work, parents/carers of children and young people with a visual impairment, and voluntary sector organisations. The site provides advice and resources for parents/carers and young people and professionals. It now hosts and is updating the pages on eye conditions formerly held by the Scottish Sensory Centre.
Vision Support Team	Local Authorities have a legal obligation to provide educational support to children and young people with vision impairment. These teams usually comprise QTVIs, specialist TAs and Habilitation Specialists. Sometimes these services are provided by outside organisations under contract, but should still be listed in the LA Local Offer pages.
Wales	Legislation and schooling in Wales is similar to that in England. Wales currently uses the **Statement of Special Educational Needs**, although SEN is changing to **Additional Learning Needs (ALN)** and each child will have an **Individual Development Plan (IDP)** although this has not been introduced at the time of writing. Foundation phase continues until the end of Year 3 See the grid at the end of the document for comparisons of school years in different nations.
Wikki Stix®	Reusable flexible waxed strands that can be moulded into shapes or pressed onto a page to produce raised pictures. Wikki Stix® offer constructive and imaginative play. They are safe, non-toxicand durable. www.youtube.com/watch?v =1Fi5OxMs1yo
WonderBaby	WonderBaby.org is dedicated to helping parents of young children with visual impairments as well as children with multiple disabilities. Despite the name it is still of value for older children. The website has sections on toys and recreation, growth and development, Braille and literacy, sensory activities, iPads and apps, and orientation and mobility: www.wonderbaby.org/
World Health Organization (WHO)	WHO works worldwide to promote health, keep the world safe, and serve the vulnerable. www.who.int/

AGE	ENGLAND – School	ENGLAND – Year	ENGLAND – Key Stage	NORTHERN IRELAND – Year	SCOTLAND – School	SCOTLAND – Year	WALES – Phase	WALES – Year	IRELAND/ÉIRE – School	IRELAND/ÉIRE – Class/year	USA – School	USA – Grade	AUSTRALIA
0–4	Pre-School	-	-			Nursery	Foundation phase					-	
4–5	Primary School (Infants)	Reception	-	1	Primary School	P1	Foundation phase	Reception	Primary School	Junior Infants		Pre-K	
5–6	"	1	KS1	2	"	P2	Foundation phase	1	"	Senior infants	Elementary	Kindergarten	Kindergarten
6–7	"	2	=	3	"	P3	Foundation phase	2	"	1st Class	Elementary	1	1
7–8	Primary School (Juniors)	3	KS2	4	"	P4	Foundation phase	3	"	2nd Class	Elementary	2	2
8–9	"	4	=	5	"	P5		4	"	3rd Class	Elementary	3	3
9–10	"	5	=	6	"	P6		5	"	4th Class	Elementary	4	4
10–11	"	6	=	7	"	P7		6	"	5th Class	Elementary	5	5
11–12	Secondary School	7	KS3	8	Secondary School	S1		7	"	6th Class	Junior High	6	6
12–13	"	8	=	9	"	S2		8	Secondary School (Junior Cycle)	1st Year	Junior High	7	7
13–14	"	9	=	10	"	S3		9	"	2nd Year	Junior High	8	8
14–15	Secondary School – GCSE	10	KS4	11	National 5s	S4		10	"	3rd Year	High School – Freshman	9	9
15–16	"	11	=	12	National 5s	S5		11	Transition year	4th Year optional transition year	High School – Sophomore	10	10
16–17	School 6th Form or College	12	A Level	13	Optional year Scottish Highers	S6		12	Secondary School (Senior Cycle)	5th Year	High School – Junior	11	11
17–18	"	13	=	14	Advanced Highers	-		13	6th Year	6th Year	High School – Senior	12	12

Further Reading

CHILD DEVELOPMENT AND THE BRAIN

Meggitt, Carolyn (2012) *Child Development: An Illustrated Guide*, 3rd edition [with DVD]. Harlow: Pearson Education.

Includes basic information on theories of child development. 2nd edition covers birth to 16 years.

Morgan, Nicola (2005/2013) *Blame My Brain: The Amazing Teenage Brain Revealed*. Walker Books.

The biology and psychology of teenage behaviour.

Singh, Ranj (2022) *Brain Power: A Toolkit to Understand and Train Your Unique Brain*. Wren and Rook.

A child friendly explanation of how the brain works for reading ages 7–9.

> https://health.usnews.com/health-news/family-health/brain-and-behavior/articles/2008/11/26/how-to-deploy
> -the-amazing-power-of-the-teen-brain

EYES AND VISION

Bowman, Richard, Bowman, Ruth and Dutton, Gordon (2010) *Disorders of Vision in Children* [CD-ROM]. London: RNIB.

https://www.vincyp.scot.nhs.uk/medical-information/

A detailed list of eye conditions from the Scottish Sensory Centre. The medical information documents were originally developed for VIScotland and are in the process of being updated by VINCYP. Visual Impairment Network for Children & Young People-Scotland.

INDEPENDENT LIVING SKILLS/ EXPANDED CORE CURRICULUM/ SPECIALIST SKILLS

Allman, Carol B. and Lewis, Sandra (2014) *ECC Essentials: Teaching the Expanded Core Curriculum to Students with Visual Impairments*.

The first comprehensive book for teachers of students with visual impairments to focus on the nine areas of the ECC that encompass the unique skills children and adolescents with visual impairments need to learn in order to access the core educational curriculum and become independent individuals.

Broadley, Fiona (2020) *Supporting Life Skills for Young Children with Vision Impairment and Other Disabilities: An Early Years Habilitation Handbook*. Speechmark.

This book offers a wealth of guidance and activities to develop children's independent living skills. Aimed at children and young people working at a lower stage as well as early years.

RNIB, University of Birmingham, VIEW and Thomas Pocklington Trust (2022) *The Curriculum Framework for Children and Young People with Vison Impairment (CFVI)*. RNIB, University of Birmingham, VIEW and Thomas Pocklington Trust.

It defines specialist skills and best and inclusive practice for children and young people with vision impairment across the UK. Downloadable from .

PARENTING

Ockwell-Smith, Sarah (2021) *Between: A Guide for Parents of Eight to Thirteen-Year-Olds*. Piatkus.

A unique blend of biology, psychology and sociology of adolescence as the basis for practical parenting advice that you can use to help your child through the transition from childhood to adulthood.

https://raisingchildren.net.au/teens/development/social-emotional-development

PUBERTY

Fisher, Nick (2013) *Living with a Willy: The Inside Story*. Macmillan Children's Books.

Practical honest and serious in all the right parts, funny and engaging in others.

Frith, Alex (2013) *What's Happening to Me?*, Boys edition. Usborne Books.

Detailed and sensitive guide to male puberty. It tackles key subjects from the physical changes that occur at this time to the emotional upheaval this can cause.

Mason, Paul (2011) *From Armpits to Zits: The Book of Yucky Body Bits*.

Full of humorous illustrations and text, this book seeks to explain and demystify the strange, and sometimes disgusting, actions of the human body.

Meredith, Susan (2006) *What's Happening to Me?*, Girls edition. Usborne Books.

A sensitive, informative guide to puberty for girls, tackles everything from body image to mood swings, hormones and first bras.

Taylor, Sonya Renee. *Celebrate Your Body (And Its Changes, Too) - A Body-Positive Guide for Girls 8+*.

Todnem, Scott (2019) *Growing Up Great!: The Ultimate Puberty Book for Boys*. Rockridge Press.

Winston, Robert (2017) *Help Your Kids with Growing Up*. Dorling Kindersley.

Demistifies puberty and other tricky issues. Written in an accessible style and suitable for parents and young people.

SOCIAL SKILLS AND EMOTIONAL WELLBEING

Download accessible books and tactile images from https://www.rnibbookshare.org/.

Kelly, Alex and Sains, Brian (2009) *Talkabout for Teenagers, Developing social and Emotional Communication Skills*. Routledge.

Offers a hierarchical approach to teaching social skills and includes assessment and activities to work on social skills.

O'Malley, Stella (2022) *Bully-Proof Kids*. Swift Press.

A practical tool kit to help children be confident, resilient and strong.

O'Neill, Poppy (2018) *You're a Star: A Guide to Self- Esteem*. Vie.

Purkis, Jeanette and Goodall, Emma (2018) *The Parents' Practical Guide to Resilience for Preteens and Teenagers on the Autism Spectrum*. Jessica Kingsley.

Sacks, Sharon Z. and Wolffe, Karen E. (2006) *Teaching Social Skills to Students with Visual Impairments: From Theory to Practice*. American Printing House for the Blind.

Schroeder, Alison (1998) *Socially Speaking: Pragmatic Social Skills Programme for Primary Pupils with Mild to Moderate Learning Disabilities*. LDA.

Practical resource for social skills lessons. Lends itself well to working with students with vision impairments. A supporting socially Speaking Game is also available.

FOOD PREPARATION

DK (2018) *Cooking Step By Step: More than 50 Delicious Recipes for Young Cooks (DK Activities)*. DK Dorling Kindersley.

Ibbs, Katharine and Saunders, Catherine (2004) *Children's Cookbook: Delicious Step-by-Step Recipes*. DK Dorling Kindersley.

TRANSITION

Burton, Matthew (2020) *Go Big. The Secondary School Survival Guide*. Wren and Rook.

Written in a child friendly format to allay the fears of students transferring to secondary school.

https://www.pocklington-trust.org.uk/student-support/secondary-school/six-steps-for-getting-ready-to-start -secondary-school/ Thomas Pocklington guidance on getting ready for secondary school

https://www.bbc.co.uk/bitesize/tags/zh4wy9q/starting-secondary-school/1 BBC bitesize information on starting secondary

https://www.bbc.co.uk/bitesize/articles/znncpg8 preparing your child for secondary school

https://youngminds.org.uk/resources/school-resources/?f2=10143#listing resources for schools supporting students through transition to secondary

Bibliography

Daniel, Goleman (2009) *Emotional Intelligence, Why it Can Matter More than IQ*, 1st edition. Bloomsbury Publishing.

Gallahue, David L. and Ozmun, John C. (2006) *Understanding Motor Development: Infants, Children, Adolescents, Adults*, 6th edition. London: McGraw-Hill.

Gogtay, N., Giedd, J.N., Lusk, L., Hayashi, K.M., Greenstein, D., Vaituzis, A.C., Nugent III, T.F., Herman, D.H., Clasen, L.S., Toga, A.W. and Rapoport, J.L. (2004) 'Dynamic mapping of human cortical development during childhood through early adulthood.' *Proceedings of the National Academy of Sciences*, 101(21), 8174–8179.

Hewett, R., Douglas, G., Ramli, A. and Keil, S. (2012) *Post-14 Transitions – A Survey of the Social Activity and Social Networking of Blind and Partially Sighted Young People: Technical Report.* VICTAR.

McLinden, M., Douglas, G., Cobb, R., Hewett, R. and Ravenscroft, J. (2016) ''Access to learning' and 'learning to access': Analysing the distinctive role of specialist teachers of children and young people with vision impairments in facilitating curriculum access through an ecological systems theory.' *British Journal of Visual Impairment*, 34(2), 177–195. https://doi.org/10.1177/0264619616643180

Ravenscroft, John, et al. (2020) *The Routledge Handbook of Visual Impairment.* Routledge.

Sacks, Sharon Z. and Wolffe, Karen E. (2006) *Teaching Social Skills to Students with Visual Impairments: From Theory to Practice.* American Printing House for the Blind.

UK Government (2014) *Special Educational Needs and Disability Code of Practice: 0 to 25 Years: Statutory Guidance for Organisations Which Work with and Support Children and Young People Who Have Special Educational Needs or Disabilities.* Department for Education and Department of Health.

https://assets.publishing.service.gov.uk/government/uploads/system/uploads/attachment_data/file/398815/SEND_Code_of_Practice_January_2015.pdf

UNICEF (2011) *Children's Wellbeing in UK, Sweden and Spain: The Role of Inequality and Materialism.* Ipsos MORI Child Wellbeing Report.

WEBSITES

Department for Education/Department of Health (2015) *Special Educational Needs and Disability Code of Practice: 0 to 25 Years*, January. London: DfE/DoH. https://assets.publishing.service.gov.uk/government/uploads/system/uploads/attachment_data/file/398815/SEND_Code_of_Practice_January_2015.pdf

Statutory guidance for organisations which work with and support children and young people who have special educational needs or disabilities.

Webster, Jerry (2019, 30 January) 'Chaining forward and chaining backwards.' *ThoughtCo*, 30 January 2019. www.thoughtco.com/chaining-forward-and-chaining-backwards-3110581

https://health.usnews.com/health-news/family-health/brain-and-behavior/articles/2008/11/26/how-to-deploy-the-amazing-power-of-the-teen-brain, accessed 11 October 2021

https://www.bl.uk/people/albert-mehrabian Information from the British Library about Albert Mehrabian and the *The 7-38-55% Communication Rule*, accessed 25 September 2021

OTHER ONLINE RESOURCES

Information about Vision Impairment: Guide for Parents. London: RNIB. https://www.rnib.org.uk/sites/default/files/APDF-ENG021603_Early%20Support%20Parents%20Information.pdf

Teaching and Learning Guidance. London: RNIB. https://www.rnib.org.uk/health-social-care-and-education-professionals/education-professionals/teaching-and-learning-guidance

https://www.vincyp.scot.nhs.uk/, accessed 26 October 2021

https://www.preparingforadulthood.org.uk/downloads/education-health-and-care-planning/pfa-outcomes-tool.htm

The Department for Education have developed an outcomes tool that is designed to support the development of PfA outcomes in EHC plans across the age range. It explores the key indicators for preparing for adulthood at different ages and stages of development.